Communications
in Computer and Information Science   1272

More information about this series at http://www.springer.com/series/7899

Onn Shehory · Eitan Farchi ·
Guy Barash (Eds.)

Engineering Dependable and Secure Machine Learning Systems

Third International Workshop, EDSMLS 2020
New York City, NY, USA, February 7, 2020
Revised Selected Papers

 Springer

Editors
Onn Shehory (iD)
Bar-Ilan University
Ramat Gan, Israel

Guy Barash (iD)
Bar-Ilan University
Ramat Gan, Israel

Eitan Farchi
IBM Haifa Research Lab
Haifa, Israel

ISSN 1865-0929   ISSN 1865-0937   (electronic)
Communications in Computer and Information Science
ISBN 978-3-030-62143-8   ISBN 978-3-030-62144-5   (eBook)
https://doi.org/10.1007/978-3-030-62144-5

This Springer imprint is published by the registered company Springer Nature Switzerland AG
The registered company address is: Gewerbestrasse 11, 6330 Cham, Switzerland

Preface

Contemporary software systems increasingly encompass machine learning (ML) components. In similarity to other software systems, ML-based software systems must meet dependability, security, and quality requirements. Standard notions of software quality and reliability such as deterministic functional correctness, black box testing, code coverage, and traditional software debugging may become irrelevant for ML systems. This is due to their non-deterministic nature, their reuse of high-quality implementations of ML algorithms, and the lack of understanding of the semantics of learned models, e.g., when deep learning methods are applied. This calls for novel methods and new methodologies and tools to address quality, security, and reliability challenges of ML software systems.

Broad deployment of ML software in interconnected systems inevitably exposes the ML software to attacks. While classical security vulnerabilities are relevant, ML techniques have additional weaknesses, some already known (e.g., sensitivity to data manipulation) and some yet to be discovered. Hence, there is a need for research as well as practical solutions to ML adversarial attacks.

The AAAI 2020 Workshop on Engineering Dependable and Secure Machine Learning Systems (EDSMLS 2020) focused on such topics. It included original contributions exposing problems and offering solutions related to dependability and quality assurance of ML software systems. It additionally included studies on adversarial attacks on such ML software systems. The workshop combined disciplines such as adversarial ML and software engineering, with emphasis on quality assurance. It also promoted a discourse between academia and industry in a quest for well-founded practical solutions.

The EDSMLS 2020 workshop was the third edition in the EDSMLS series. It was held on February 7, 2020, as part of AAAI 2020, in New York City, USA. The event was well attended by researchers from academia and industry. The presentations addressed adversarial ML, reliable ML, secure ML, and the relationships between them. The presentations, and discussions that followed, were very lively, fertile, and inspiring, leading to new future research on adversarial, reliable, and secure ML.

The EDSMLS 2020 program included 11 presentations, of which 1 was an invited keynote and 10 were of peer-reviewed, accepted papers, selected out of 16 submissions. Each paper was peer-reviewed by at least two Program Committee members. To further improve their quality, all post-proceedings papers have undergone another review round by two reviewers each and were accepted to this volume once they had been revised, addressing reviewers' comments. The reviews in both review rounds were single blind.

The papers included in this volume present state-of-the-art research in the study of reliable, dependable, and adversarial ML software systems. The volume includes very recent results, some of which call for further research and expansion. EDSMLS organizers are confident that the problems and solutions presented here shall serve as a fertile ground for future research in this growing field.

August 2020

Eitan Farchi
Onn Shehory
Guy Barash

Organization

General Chairs

Onn Shehory   Bar-Ilan University, Israel
Guy Barash   Western Digital, Israel
Eitan Farchi   IBM Research Haifa, Israel

Program Committee

Eitan Farchi   IBM Research Haifa, Israel
Onn Shehory   Bar-Ilan University, Israel
Guy Barash   Western Digital, Israel
Maria Spichkova   RMIT University, Australia
Sailik Sengupta   Arizona State University, USA
Oded Margalit   IBM Cyber Security Center of Excellence (CCoE),
                                 Israel
Orna Raz   IBM Research Haifa, Israel
Jan Olaf Blech   RMIT University, Australia
Peter Santhanam   IBM Research NY, USA
Lei Cui   Beihang University, China
Victor Pankratius   MIT, USA
Pratik Vaishnavi   Stony Brook University, USA
Samuel Marchal   Aalto University, Finland

Contents

Quality Management of Machine Learning Systems

P. Santhanam$^{(\boxtimes)}$

IBM Research AI, T.J. Watson Research Center, Yorktown Heights, NY, USA
pasanth@us.ibm.com

Abstract. In the past decade, Artificial Intelligence (AI) has become a part of our daily lives due to major advances in Machine Learning (ML) techniques. In spite of an explosive growth in the raw AI technology and in consumer facing applications on the internet, its adoption in business applications has conspicuously lagged behind. For business/mission-critical systems, serious concerns about reliability and maintainability of AI applications remain. Due to the statistical nature of the output, software 'defects' are not well defined. Consequently, many traditional quality management techniques such as program debugging, static code analysis, functional testing, etc. have to be reevaluated. Beyond the correctness of an AI model, many other new quality attributes, such as fairness, robustness, explainability, transparency, etc. become important in delivering an AI system. The purpose of this paper is to present a view of a holistic quality management framework for ML applications based on the current advances and identify new areas of software engineering research to achieve a more trustworthy AI.

Keywords: Artificial Intelligence · Machine learning · Quality management · AI Engineering

1 Introduction

According to the 2019 AI Index report [1], hundreds of papers are published on AI technology every day! In 18 months, the time required to train a large image classification system on the cloud infrastructure has fallen from about 3 h to about 88 s! In 2019, global private AI investment was over \$70B. In 2018, the State of California licensed testing of more than 500 autonomous vehicles, which drove over 2 million miles. When it comes to real AI applications, many companies on the internet use the latest machine learning techniques to perform various consumer facing tasks, such as, answer questions, recognize images, recommend products, translate content, etc. Not a day goes by when there is not a news report of a new application of machine learning to some new domain. All these trends point to an explosion of AI related technology all around.

Interestingly, the adoption of AI in the enterprise for business critical applications has lagged considerably behind. Recent analysts reports from various

© Springer Nature Switzerland AG 2020
O. Shehory et al. (Eds.): EDSMLS 2020, CCIS 1272, pp. 1–13, 2020.
https://doi.org/10.1007/978-3-030-62144-5_1

sources [2] indicate at most 20–40% success rate for the adoption of AI to create business value. This supports the assertion that moving AI from a proof-of-concept to real business solution is not a trivial exercise. Some common reasons cited for this result are:

- Insufficient alignment of business goals and processes to the AI technology (akin to the challenges of introducing information technology in the 1990's).
- Lack of data strategy (i.e. "There is no AI without IA (Information Architecture)")
- Shortage of skilled people who can combine domain knowledge and the relevant AI technology.
- Unique concerns about AI (e.g. model transparency, explainability, fairness/bias, reliability, safety, maintenance, etc.)
- Need for better engineering infrastructure for data and model provenance.

As the application of AI moves to business/mission critical tasks with more severe consequences, the need for a rigorous quality management framework becomes critical. It is bound to be very different from the practices and processes that have been in place for IT projects over many decades. The goal of this paper is to provide an overview of such a framework built upon tools and methodology available today and identify gaps for new software engineering research. The focus of this paper is on AI systems implemented using machine learning. A popular ML technique is the use of Deep Neural Networks (DNN). This paper uses AI and ML interchangeably.

2   AI Is Software

In general, the use of an AI component has one of three goals. (i) automate an existing task performed by a human e.g. Support Bots (ii) improve the efficiency of an existing task e.g. language translation (iii) perform a new task e.g. a recommender system. The invocation of the AI is through traditional interfaces (e.g. REST based microservices). In this respect, it is just another software component, albeit with some special attributes. Thus, from the system or software management point of view, it has all the same expectations as any other software component. Figure 1 shows the recommended system and software quality models and attributes from the ISO/IEC 25010 process standard [3]. Reference [4] gives an accessible overview of the relevant attributes. Even though the specific interpretation may have to be refined for the purpose of AI components, the utility of the basic structure is immediately evident. The quality attributes in use (in the left column) i.e. effectiveness, efficiency, satisfaction, risk and context coverage do represent the relevant dimensions for consideration. Inclusion of 'Trust' under the 'Satisfaction' category is fortuitous in hindsight, since it has taken a more profound meaning for AI components. The product quality attributes on the right are essential for product owners. Notably, the common metric used by AI algorithm owners is accuracy which relates to 'Functional Correctness' in Fig. 1 and it is only one of the more than two dozen attributes in the ISO standard. *It is important to evaluate an AI component against these attributes to understand the requirements they place on the use of an AI component in a software system.*

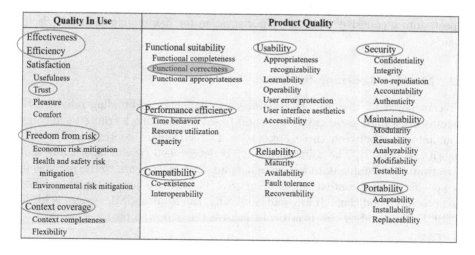

Fig. 1. ISO/IEC 25010- system and software quality models [3,4]

2.1 Traditional Software Quality Management

The engineering practices for managing software quality go back many decades [5], and McConnell [6] gives a more recent view of practices and tools. A key assumption is that **expected functional behavior (i.e. linking inputs and outputs) of components is documented (or understood) at design time**, even if design evolves during a project. Central to quality management is the definition of a **defect** (aka bug) as the software behavior not meeting the expectation. Defects can be opened during any of the development activities [7], namely, Design or Code Review, Unit Test (white box), Function Test (black box), System Test (integration), and during DevOps or Operations.

There are seven aspects to managing quality processes in a software project. (i) **Requirements management** that evaluates the incoming (and often changing) requirements and selects the requirements for inclusion in the upcoming software release(s). (ii) **Defect management** which includes the process of opening, debugging, fixing, closing and counting defects across the life cycle. (iii) **Change management**, which relates to versioning and tracking of changes to code and documentation during the life cycle. (iv) **Test Management**, consisting of Test design, Test creation, Test execution and Evaluation metrics (e.g. test effectiveness, defect density, code or functional coverage, etc.) This applies across all levels of testing i.e. unit testing (white box), function testing (black box), etc. (v) **Dev/Op processes** that manage the promotion of code from development to operations with the necessary processes and automation (e.g. regression tests) to validate deployment quality and support the run-time environment. (vi) **Operations management** that collects incident reports during operations and provides a mechanism for support teams to diagnose and resolve them expediently, which may involve the original engineers who created the relevant code. (vii) **Project management** that brings these six different aspects into a cohesive decision support system for risk management via dashboards.

2.2 Machine Learning Systems

A recent paper [8] discusses the engineering challenges in building reliable ML systems. At a high level, any AI solution based on machine learning technology is an interplay between three factors i.e. Data, Domain context and the AI Algorithms (Fig. 2). The solution quality is determined by the algorithms that learn from the training data to create outputs that make sense to the humans in the specific domain context/application area. These three factors together define the necessary conditions. If any one is missing, the resulting ML system is likely to fail. Understanding this is critical to assess the expected business value of an AI system.

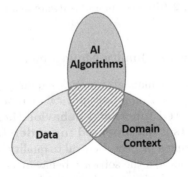

Fig. 2. Critical success factors for AI applications

In supervised machine learning, the modeling data consists of large number of inputs and the corresponding outputs (called labels). The main goal of the ML algorithm is to find the best approximation to the function that maps the inputs to the output(s). During inference, the output is the prediction that can be a continuous variable (e.g. price of a stock or tomorrow's temperature) or a label/class (e.g. predicting the next word in a search engine, identifying an image as a cat, etc.) These ML functions do not have a requirement/specification document at the design time; they are just derived from the modeling data. Model outputs are statistical and not deterministic. Consequently, there is no simple way to define a defect! As an example, an image recognition algorithm may identify a 'cat' as a 'dog' for some of the instances and this is allowed by

Table 1. Key perspectives in quality management of AI projects

Activity	Key AI Perspectives
Requirement Management	• Is the choice of AI task appropriate to meet the business objective? • Does the relevant modeling data exist in quality and quantity? • Are there specific plans to manage Trust?
Defect Management	• Is the accuracy of the model adequate for the purpose? • Debugging support to resolve algorithm vs. data
Change Management	• Versioning of models and the appropriate data • Tracking models during Active Learning at run time
Test Management	• Cross validation during model building • Hold out data sets during black box testing • Validating Trust expectations
DevOps	• Versioning of models and the appropriate data for each build • Ability to do differential diagnosis of model performance across builds
Operations Management	• Monitoring operations for model drifts • Debugging issues found during operations back to the model inadequacies
Project Management	• Managing the application lifecycle vs. model lifecycle • Data management strategy • Assessing business goals vs. AI performance • Managing Trust expectations • Need for maintaining the project IT infrastructure for the life of the application

the statistical uncertainties in the algorithm. Debugging is complicated since the problem can be in the model and/or the data. No guarantees or explanations are provided on the exact functional operations of the model. Traditional testing will not work, since there is no description of the expected behavior at design time. In addition, ML Model behavior can drift over time during deployment due to previously unseen data. If the model is learning continuously during deployment, new patterns of relationships in data can emerge, unknown to the model owners.

The potential breadth of AI applications invokes serious social concerns as evidenced by various government initiatives such as the European Commission Ethics Guidelines for Trustworthy AI [9] and AI Ethics Principles for the US Department of Defense [10]. Any AI quality management framework has to address these concerns. Table 1 describes the changes to the quality processes discussed in Sect. 2.1 due to the inclusion of an AI component. It is clear that **every one of the traditional quality management activities is affected.** Due to the nature of the AI applications, the quality management is a required and never ending activity, as long as the application is in use.

3   A Quality Management Framework for ML Systems

The purpose of this section is to identify the key components that are needed to have an adequate quality management framework for successful delivery of reliable ML systems. Some of the components have prototype technology already available for use, but while others need more experimentation and new research. This discussion leverages some of the concepts from references [11–14].

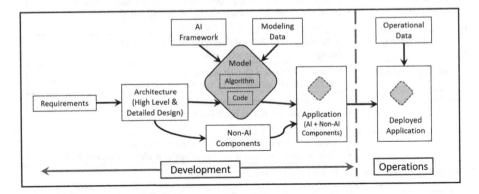

Fig. 3. Key artifacts in the creation of an application with one ML component implemented in the model (gray rounded square). For simplicity, iterative process steps are not shown and only the AI component properties are emphasized.

Figure 3 shows the key artifacts in the development of a ML application. For simplicity, we emphasize AI specific artifacts. All software projects start with a set of functional and non-functional requirements, mostly in natural language documents. Software architecture consists of high level and detailed designs typically captured in various diagrams [6]. Detailed designs identify the specific functions needed for the implementation. One or more of the functions can be implemented by data scientists using ML models. Modeling data refers to the data available for training and validation. The data scientists either reuse algorithms and other components from popular AI frameworks (e.g. TensorFlow, PyTorch, etc.) or write the modeling code for the first time. Model gets integrated with other non-AI components (e.g. user interface, traditional analytics, reporting, etc.) and IT components (e.g. access control) to create the business application which is subsequently deployed to operations.

3.1 Where Are the Bugs?

The defects in application requirements and design are nothing new in software development, but ML introduces some twists in the assessment of the right task for the automation with AI, based on business expectations on quality (discussed above) and operational performance. Incorrect choice of algorithm for the chosen task is a common source for quality concerns. The programming errors in the implementation of the algorithm is also not a new problem. Examples are incorrect API calls, syntax errors, incorrect model parameter, etc. These can be addressed with additional support from the frameworks, much like Eclipse for Java.

As in all projects that involve statistics, the quality and quantity of the available data are major concerns. An example of raw data quality is "expectation mismatch" (i.e. incorrect data type for feature values, Non-boolean value for boolean feature type, etc.) The more subtle data problems relate to noisy labels in the modeling data and issues with data distributions (e.g. the fraction of examples containing a feature is too small, data distribution is different for training and validation data sets, etc.) Data problems also resurface in production when the operational data profile does not match the data used during model development or due to unexpected emergent behavior.

Due to the extensive use of open source machine learning frameworks (i.e. TensorFlow, CNTK, Keras, Theano, PyTorch, etc.) and associated libraries, they become additional sources of bugs [15,16]. Testing a ML library for a specific algorithm (e.g. convolutional neural network, recurrent neural network, etc.) will require implementation of the same algorithm in different ML libraries and luckily this is not a problem with common algorithms and popular libraries. Examples of bugs in frameworks are: not backward compatible API versions, unaligned tensors, pooling scheme inconsistency, etc.

Then, there are the bugs in the model itself, as evidenced by an unexpected output for the given input (e.g. a cat's image identified as a dog), through various modeling errors such as overfitting, unoptimized hyper parameters, wrong neural net architecture, etc. Once the model is integrated into the business application, the defects in the ML components get mixed up with the traditional software defects in the other components. The overall quality of the application is obviously dependent on all the contributing software components, such as user interface, back end management, etc.

3.2   Quality Improvement Tasks for ML Systems

This section describes the suggested tasks to find defects in the artifacts described in Sect. 3.1 and resolve them. These are traditional activities modified to reflect the inclusion of the ML component in the application. *Due to space limitations, reference to any specific technique or tool is meant to provide an example, rather than an exhaustive list.* Quality improvement tasks that address the unique aspects of assessing 'Trust' in ML systems are described in Sect. 3.3.

Manual Inspection. With the support of tools [17] manual inspection is still an effective way to find defects in requirements, architecture, algorithms and code. Techniques, such as pair programming [6] have proven very useful in practice.

Static Analysis. Application of static analysis to find defects in software programs is a very mature field, dating back to many decades [18]. There have been recent examples of applying this technique to machine learning code [19]. Many development environments support basic syntax checking, when the code is being written.

White Box Testing. Traditional white box testing [20] leverages the knowledge of the program structure to execute the program in ways to achieve the desired coverage e.g. branch coverage, statement coverage, etc. to locate defects. Similarly, a data scientist can use the detailed knowledge of a neural network behavior in the model building process to apply various coverage criteria to the network to find the defects in the model. This has led to concepts such as neuron coverage [21], novel test criteria that are tailored to structural features of DNNs and their semantics [22], the condition-decision relationships between adjacent layers and the combinations of values of neurons in the same layer [23], mutation techniques on source code, data and models [24] and combinatorial test design consisting of neuron pairs in the layers and the neuron-activation configurations[25]. These techniques demonstrate various ways to expose incorrect behavior of the network while being mindful of the computational cost of test generation itself.

Black Box Testing. Traditional black box testing (or functional testing) [20] focuses on detecting defects in the expected external behavior of the software component by carefully manipulating the input space. For ML models, it is important that test data represents the business requirements in terms of data values and distributions and was not used during the model creation process. Key goal of black box testing is to evaluate if the model generalizes adequately for previously unseen data or suggest a model rework, if not suitable. These considerations also apply for system integration tests.

Data Assessment and Testing. There are several techniques and tools to check the quality of the modeling data during development. Breck et al. [26] present a highly scalable data validation system, designed to detect data anomalies (e.g. unexpected patterns, schema-free data, etc.) in the machine learning pipelines. Barash et al. [27] use combinatorial design methodology to define the space of business requirements and map it to the ML solution data, and use the notion of data slices to identify uncovered requirements, under-performing slices, or suggest the need for additional training data. This is also an example of using data slicing for black box testing.

Application Monitoring. Application monitoring during operations is a critical activity in ML applications since the model performance can change over time due to previously unseen pattern in the operational data or emergent behavior not expected in the model building process. Breck et al. [26] also describe techniques to detect feature skew by doing a key-join between corresponding batches of training and operational data followed by a feature wise comparison. Distribution skew between training data and serving data is detected by distance measures. Raz et al. [28] discuss a novel approach, solely based on a classifier suggested labels and its confidence in them, for alerting on data distribution or feature space changes that are likely to cause data drift. This has two distinct benefits viz. no model input data is required and does not require labeling of data in production. In addition to the detecting any degradation of model performance, there need to be processes in place to correct the behavior as and when it occurs. There are examples of commercial offerings to perform this task [29].

Debugging. Debugging is often the most under-appreciated activity in software development that takes considerable skill and effort in reality. As noted in [7], debugging typically happens during three different stages in software life cycle, and the level of granularity of the analysis required for locating the defect differs in these three. First stage is during the model building process by the data scientist who has access to the details of the model. Here, there are two classes of errors that need debugging. (a) raw errors resulting in the execution of the model code in the development environment during the process of model creation. The development frameworks can provide support for debugging this class of problems. (b) Model executes successfully, but the overall performance of the model output is not adequate for the chosen task or if the model output does not meet the expectation for specific input instances, it is necessary to find the reason for these behaviors. There could be many causes, including bad choice of the algorithm, inadequate tuning of the parameters, quality and quantity of the modeling data, etc. [30,31]. Some care is also needed in providing model debugging information to the user to avoid exposure of system details, susceptible for adversarial attacks.

The second stage for debugging is during the later black box testing activities in development when an unexpected behavior is encountered. A certain amount of debugging of the test execution is necessary to conclude that the AI model is the cause of the unexpected behavior. Once that is confirmed, debugging of the model follows the same process as described above. Third stage is during operations, when the application is being put to real use. Any unexpected behavior here can be the result of changes in the computing environment relative to development or due to new patterns in the operational data not previously seen the modeling data. Techniques discussed in [26,28,29] can be used to address the model drift problems.

3.3   AI Trust Assessment

Due to the black box nature of the ML models and their behavior being decided by modeling data, trust in model outputs has become an important consideration in business applications. This section deals with four specific aspects trust.

Explainability. In many business critical applications, the outputs of the black box ML models also require explanations to meet the business objectives. There are many motivations for explanations [32] and it is important to know the need so that the appropriate approach can be used. There are examples of open source packages for implementing explainability [33] in business applications.

Bias/Fairness. Due to the potential sensitivity of the outputs of the ML models to biases inherent in the modeling data, there is a critical question of the fairness of the algorithms [34] in extracting the model from the data. There are examples of open source packages for understanding and mitigating biases [35] in business applications.

Robustness. The owner of a ML application needs a strategy for defending against adversarial attacks. Xu et al. [36] provide a comprehensive summary of the adversarial attacks against ML models built using images, graphs and text and the countermeasures available. Reference [37] describes an open-source software library, designed to help researchers and developers in creating novel defense techniques, and in deploying practical defenses of real-world AI systems.

Transparency. Given the abundance of AI components (i.e. algorithms, services, libraries, frameworks) available from open source and commercial offerings, it makes sense for a company to reuse the available software component in its application. However, due to the concerns about the trust in the available component, the consumer of the component needs some detailed information about the component to manage the risk. This need for transparency requires additional assessment. Key pieces of such information are captured in a FactSheet [38], which provides the technical and process background of the AI asset to the consumer.

3.4   Quality Metrics

Due to the unique attributes of AI based systems (discussed in Sect. 2), there is a critical need to reevaluate the metrics for their quality management. This section discusses three aspects that highlight the need.

Defect Management. The lack of a clear definition of software defect in ML applications discussed in Sect. 2.2 is a major problem in quality management. While the defects in the other artifacts can be captured unambiguously, the perceived errors in the model outputs are subject to the statistical uncertainties. As a result, until a detailed debugging is performed to diagnose the reason for the unexpected behavior one cannot be certain that this is a bug. Hence the defect management tools have to allow this possibility with potentially more time assigned for the necessary investigation that may point to an inadequate training data set.

Model Evaluation. Model evaluation is an important part of the ML application development. There are many metrics [39] that can be used and depending on the specific application domain. They need to be chosen and used carefully. In addition to these usual machine learning metrics, additional metrics specific to the trust topics discussed in Sect. 3.3 (explainability, bias, robustness and transparency) are also necessary to support the business objectives and manage technical & business risk. There is also recent work [40] to measure application-level key performance indicators to provide feedback to the AI model life cycle.

Model Uncertainty. In addition to the usual ML metrics [39], typically at the end of a DNN pipeline is a softmax activation that estimates a confidence level for each output, expressed as a probability measure between 0 and 1. In reality, a high confidence level does not necessarily mean low uncertainty [41] and hence it is not reliable for decision support. This is because DNN models do not have a way of calculating uncertainty by themselves. Gal and Ghahramani [41] have proposed a new method to estimate uncertainty in DNN outputs that approximates Bayesian models, while not requiring a high computing cost. Lakshminarayanan et al. [42] have demonstrated an alternate approach that is scalable and can be easily implemented. Any mission critical ML system has to include such uncertainty measures.

4 Conclusions

The purpose of this paper is to discuss a framework for a quality management system needed to support the inclusion of AI components in the building of business/mission critical applications. It should be clear from the description above, that ML applications need a different mindset from the start of a project. Since AI is really a software component, we need to apply the relevant software quality attributes to it. AI comes with some special quality attributes (fairness, explainability, etc.) which have to be integrated into the quality management methodology. Various processes and tools to support the quality management of the application are in their infancy, mostly as prototypes from research projects. In addition to the raw tooling needed for each task described in Sect. 3, the integration of them across the life cycle to provide a holistic system is critical for wide scale use. Furthermore, ethical guidelines from governments [9,10] require an engineering implementation to demonstrate adherence. This does not exist today. In spite of an extraordinary worldwide effort devoted to Machine Learning technology, the quality management of AI systems is fragmented and incomplete. In order to meet the needs of society, we need an AI engineering framework that meets the rigor needed. This paper provides an early glimpse of such a framework.

Acknowledgements. Author thanks Rachel Bellamy, Evelyn Duesterwald, Eitan Farchi, Michael Hind, David Porter, Orna Raz and Jim Spohrer for useful comments on the paper.

References

1. AI Index Report. https://hai.stanford.edu/research/ai-index-2019

2. KPMG 2019 Report: "AI Transforming the Enterprise"; O' Reilly 2019 Report: "AI Adoption in the Enterprise"; Databricks 2018 Report: "Enterprise AI Adoption"; MIT Sloan-BCG Research Report "Winning With AI"
3. ISO/IEC 25010: 2011, Systems and software engineering - Systems and software Quality Requirements and Evaluation (SQuaRE) - System and software quality models
4. Codacy Blog: ISO/IEC 25010 Software Quality Model. https://blog.codacy.com/iso-25010-software-quality-model/
5. Brooks, F.P.: The Mythical Man-Month: Essays on Software Engineering, Anniversary Edition. Addison-Wesley Longman, Reading (1995)
6. McConnell, S.: Code Complete: A Practical Handbook of Software Construction, 2nd edn. Microsoft Press, Redmond (2004)
7. Hailpern, B., Santhanam, P.: Software debugging, testing and verification. IBM Syst. J. **41**, 4–12 (2002)
8. Santhanam, P., Farchi, E., Pankratius, V.: Engineering reliable deep learning systems. In: AAAI Fall Symposium Series on AI in Government & Public Sector (2019)
9. European Commission High-Level Expert Group on AI: Ethics Guidelines for Trustworthy AI. https://ec.europa.eu/futurium/en/ai-alliance-consultation
10. Defense Innovation Board: Principles: Recommendations on the Ethical Use of Artificial Intelligence by the Department of Defense (2019)
11. Beck, E., et al.: The ML test score: a rubric for ML production readiness and technical debt reduction. In: IEEE International Conference on Big Data (2017)
12. Amershi, S., et al.: Software engineering for machine learning: a case study. In: 41st International Conference on Software Engineering: Software Engineering in Practice (ICSE-SEIP 2019) (2019)
13. Zhang, J.M., et al.: Machine learning testing: survey, landscapes and horizons. arXiv:1906.10742 (2019)
14. Akkiraju, R. et al.: Characterizing machine learning process: a maturity framework. arXiv:1811.04871 (2018)
15. Zhangy, Y., et al.: An empirical study on TensorFlow program bugs. In: 27th ACM SIGSOFT International Symposium on Software Testing and Analysis (ISSTA 2018) (2018)
16. Pham, H.V., et al.: CRADLE: cross-backend validation to detect and localize bugs in deep learning libraries. In: 41st International Conference on Software Engineering (ICSE 2019) (2019)
17. Macdonald, F., et al.: A review of tool support for software inspections. In: Seventh International Workshop on Computer-Aided Software Engineering, pp. 340–349 (1995)
18. Gosain, A., Sharma, G.: Static analysis: a survey of techniques and tools. In: Mandal, D., Kar, R., Das, S., Panigrahi, B.K. (eds.) Intelligent Computing and Applications. AISC, vol. 343, pp. 581–591. Springer, New Delhi (2015). https://doi.org/10.1007/978-81-322-2268-2_59
19. Dolby, J., et al.: Ariadne: analysis for machine learning programs. In: 2nd ACM SIGPLAN International Workshop on Machine Learning and Programming Languages (MAPL 2018) (2018)
20. Nidhra, S., Dondeti, J.: Black box and white box testing techniques-a literature review. Int. J. Embed. Syst. Appl. (IJESA) **2**(2), 29–50 (2012)
21. Pei, K., et al.: DeepXplore: automated whitebox testing of deep learning systems. In: 26th ACM Symposium on Operating Systems Principles (SOSP 2017) (2017)

22. Sun, Y., et al.: Testing deep neural networks. arXiv:1803.04792v4 (2019)
23. Sekhon, J., Fleming, C.: Towards improved testing for deep learning. In: 41st International Conference on Software Engineering: New Ideas and Emerging Results (ICSE-NIER) (2019)
24. Ma, L., et al.: DeepMutation: mutation testing of deep learning systems. In: IEEE 29th International Symposium on Software Reliability Engineering (ISSRE 2018) (2018)
25. Ma, L., et al.: Combinatorial testing for deep learning systems. arXiv:1806.07723 (2018)
26. Breck, E., et al.: Data validation for machine learning. In: Second SysML Conference (2019)
27. Barash, G., et al.: Bridging the gap between ml solutions and their business requirements using feature interactions. In: 27th ACM Joint Meeting on European Software Engineering Conference and Symposium on the Foundations of Software Engineering (ESEC/FSE 2019) (2019)
28. Raz, O., et al.: Automatically detecting data drift in machine learning based classifiers. In: AAAI Workshop on Engineering Dependable and Secure Machine Learning Systems (EDSMLS 2019) (2019)
29. IBM Watson OpenScale-Drift. https://www.ibm.com/cloud/watson-openscale/drift
30. Zhang, J., et al.: Manifold: a model-agnostic framework for interpretation and diagnosis of machine learning models. IEEE Trans. Vis. Comput. Graph. **25**(1), 364–373 (2019)
31. Chakarov, A., et al.: Debugging machine learning tasks. arXiv:1603.07292v1 (2016)
32. Guidotti, R., et al.: A survey of methods for explaining black box models. ACM Comput. Surv. **51**, 1–42 (2018). Article no. 93
33. IBM Research Blog: Introducing AI Explainability 360. https://www.ibm.com/blogs/research/2019/08/ai-explainability-360/
34. Verma, S., Rubin, J.: Fairness definitions explained. In: IEEE/ACM International Workshop on Software Fairness (FairWare) (2018)
35. Bellamy, R.K.E., et al.: AI fairness 360: an extensible toolkit for detecting, understanding, and mitigating unwanted algorithmic bias. IBM J. Res. Dev. **63**(4/5) (2019)
36. Xu, H., et al.: Adversarial attacks and defenses in images, graphs and text: a review. arXiv:1909.08072 (2019)
37. IBM Research Blog: The Adversarial Robustness Toolbox: Securing AI Against Adversarial Threats. https://www.ibm.com/blogs/research/2018/04/ai-adversarial-robustness-toolbox/
38. Arnold, M. et al.: FactSheets: increasing trust in AI services through supplier's declarations of conformity. IBM J. Res. Dev. **63**(4/5) (2019)
39. Brownlee, J.: BLOG: Metrics To Evaluate Machine Learning Algorithms in Python. https://machinelearningmastery.com/metrics-evaluate-machine-learning-algorithms-python/
40. Arnold, M. et al.: Towards automating the AI operations lifecycle. In: MLOps Workshop at MLSys (2020)
41. Gal, Y., Ghahramani, Z.: Dropout as a Bayesian approximation: representing model uncertainty in deep learning. In: 33rd International Conference on Machine Learning (ICML 2016) (2016)
42. Lakshminarayanan, B., Pritzel, A., Blundell, C.: Simple and scalable predictive uncertainty estimation using deep ensembles. In: Advances in Neural Information Processing Systems 30 (NIPS 2017) (2017)

Can Attention Masks Improve Adversarial Robustness?

Pratik Vaishnavi[1]([⊠])[iD], Tianji Cong[2][iD], Kevin Eykholt[2][iD], Atul Prakash[2][iD], and Amir Rahmati[1][iD]

[1] Stony Brook University, Stony Brook, NY 11794, USA
pvaishnavi@cs.stonybrook.edu, amir@rahmati.com
[2] University of Michigan, Ann Arbor, MI 48109, USA
{congtj,keykholt,aprakash}@umich.edu

Abstract. Deep Neural Networks (DNNs) are known to be susceptible to adversarial examples. Adversarial examples are maliciously crafted inputs that are designed to fool a model, but appear normal to human beings. Recent work has shown that pixel discretization can be used to make classifiers for MNIST highly robust to adversarial examples. However, pixel discretization fails to provide significant protection on more complex datasets. In this paper, we take the first step towards reconciling these contrary findings. Focusing on the observation that discrete pixelization in MNIST makes the background completely black and foreground completely white, we hypothesize that the important property for increasing robustness is the elimination of image background using attention masks before classifying an object. To examine this hypothesis, we create foreground attention masks for two different datasets, GTSRB and MS-COCO. Our initial results suggest that using attention mask leads to improved robustness. On the adversarially trained classifiers, we see an adversarial robustness increase of over 20% on MS-COCO.

Keywords: Machine learning · Computer vision · Security

1 Introduction

Deep Neural Networks are employed in a wide range of applications ranging from autonomous systems to trading and healthcare. This has resulted in an increased attention to their security. One of the primary focuses of these efforts has been defense against adversarial examples. Adversarial examples [14] can be generated by adding carefully-crafted imperceptible noise to a normal input example. Such an adversarial example can be used to trigger a misclassification on a target model for image classification tasks (*e.g.*, a road-sign classifier in a self-driving car). Many techniques have been developed to tackle this problem [6,9,17], one of the popular one being adversarial training.

In analyzing an adversarially trained DNN on MNIST, Madry *et al.* [9] found that the first layer filters turned out to be thresholding-filters that were acting

© Springer Nature Switzerland AG 2020
O. Shehory et al. (Eds.): EDSMLS 2020, CCIS 1272, pp. 14–22, 2020.
https://doi.org/10.1007/978-3-030-62144-5_2

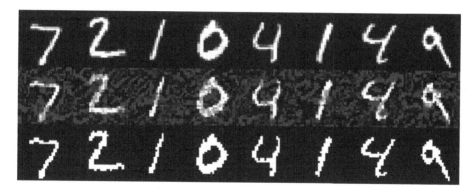

Fig. 1. Visualizing images from the MNIST dataset. The first row contains natural images, the second row contains corresponding adversarial images and the third row contains binarized adversarial images (threshold = 0.5). Binarization removes almost all the adversarial noise.

as a de-noiser for the grayscale MNIST images. Follow up experiments by Schott *et al.* [11] showed that training a DNN with binarized MNIST images (where each pixel was discretized to be either made completely black or completely white using a static threshold) resulted in significantly improved adversarial accuracy without any adversarial training or negative impact on normal performance. In other words, a pipeline that first thresholds each pixel in an MNIST image to 1 or 0 and then classifies the resulting image with a naturally trained model has a very high degree of adversarial robustness, without requiring any adversarial training. Subsequent works, however, found that a simple binarization was not effective for more complex datasets such as CIFAR-10 [3].

In contrast to previous work, we observe that binarization on MNIST acts as an approximation for the process of *foreground-background* separation. Figure 1 presents a sample image from the MNIST dataset. The MNIST dataset consists of 28×28 pixel images of handwritten white digits on a black background and are among the simplest datasets in ML. Adversarial attacks on MNIST typically do not distinguish between the digits and the background and may similarly manipulate both to achieve their goal. When examining the adversarial noise in MNIST adversarial examples for a naturally-trained model, we see that the adversarial noise is spread throughout the image, including in background regions of the image that we might not consider to carry any predictive signals. Binarization on MNIST as a pre-processing step snaps most of the background pixels back to the original value on which the model was trained (*i.e.*, 0), hence reducing the attack surface.

Therefore, it may be more accurate to characterize binarization on MNIST as foreground-background separation rather than simple pixel discretization for more complex image datasets. If the hypothesis is true, then we should see improved robustness on other datasets by simply separating the background from the foreground and masking the background prior to training and classification, i.e., applying a foreground-attention mask on the dataset.

Towards validating the above hypothesis, given a classifier and a dataset, we introduce an additional pre-processing step where a foreground attention mask is applied to the model's input before classification. A challenge in testing our hypothesis is determining the foreground attention mask. Unfortunately, most image datasets on which adversarial testing is done (e.g., CIFAR-10, ImageNet) lack sufficient ground truth data for foreground attention masks. To address the challenge, we generate two datasets with foreground attention masks from existing datasets: The German Traffic Sign Recognition (GTSRB) [13] and MS-COCO [8]. For the GTSRB dataset, we took advantage of the typical color distribution in images and that a road sign often lies in the center of the image, and used them to design a custom attention mask generator by doing random sampling of pixels near the center of the image along with a min cut-max flow algorithm to create the foreground attention mask. For the MS-COCO dataset, we use the segmentation masks included with the dataset to create a cropped image of the object of interest and its foreground mask.

Our preliminary results suggest that a classification pipeline that utilizes foreground attention masks experiences improved adversarial robustness with, at worst, no impact on natural accuracy. On the naturally trained classifiers, the adversarial accuracy improves by 0.73% on MS-COCO and around 19.69% on GTSRB. Robustness improvements were also found on combining usage of attention masks with adversarial training. Thus, this paper makes the following contributions:

- We create two datasets based on the GTSRB and MS-COCO that allow exploration of attention mask effects on adversarial examples. These datasets are available at [link].
- We take the first step toward exploring the effect of attention masks on improving model robustness in image classification tasks. We show that attention masks have certain effect on improving adversarial performance against PGD adversary.

2   Background

Discrete Pixelization Defenses. Developing adversarial defenses towards robust classification has received significant attention in recent years [7,9]. Among these, defense methods that pre-process inputs to improve robustness are potentially attractive because the pre-processed input can be passed to existing classifiers for improved robustness. Unfortunately, some of these methods were vulnerable to stronger adaptive adversarial attacks [2], raising doubts on the effectiveness of pre-processing strategies.

One pre-processing strategy that has stood attacks well against stronger adaptive adversarial attacks is that of binarization for the MNIST dataset. Unfortunately, binarization, which converts each pixel value to fewer bits did not provide a significant benefit on more complex datasets and, in some cases, negatively impacted test accuracy [3]. Chen *et al.* provide theoretical insights into the phenomenon, concluding that discrete pixelization is unlikely to provide significant benefit.

Semantic Segmentation. Semantic segmentation of images has applications in diverse fields like biomedical imaging [10]. [4,15] describe semantic segmentation techniques for complex real-word datasets like MSCOCO and Cityscapes. However, [1] have shown that DNN-based segmentation pipelines can be susceptible to adversarial attacks, though other work has shown that such attacks may be successfully detected [16], potentially providing a defense. We note that, unlike our work, prior work on robustness of semantic segmentation looked at robustness of segmentation model itself and not the impact of foreground-background separation on robustness of classification of a foreground object.

Attention Masks. According to work by Xie *et al.* on feature denoising, they discovered that adversarial noise causes machine learning models to focus on semantically uninformative information in the input, whereas the opposite is true for natural clean inputs. Thus, rather than relying on the model to identify relevant input features, we explore if we can force the network to focus on important portions of the image (*e.g.*, the foreground object). Harley *et al.* [5] proposed the idea of segmentation-aware convolution networks that rely on local attention masks, which are generated based on color-distance among neighboring pixels, and found that it can improve semantic segmentation and optical flow estimation. Our work aims to understand if attention masks can also be useful for improvement of robustness of image classification.

3   Our Approach

In this work, our goal is to examine if isolating predictive signals in the form of foreground features has benefits in terms of adversarial robustness while having minimal impact on model performance on natural inputs. We examine, using two datasets, that training a model on foreground pixels helps it perform well not only on natural images, but makes it robust against adversarial images as well.

Let $\mathbf{X}$ be a set of images drawn from a distribution. Let's consider the task of image classification defined on $\mathbf{X}$. Traditionally, in image classification, we restrict each image to contain only one object. An image $x^{(i)} \in \mathbf{X}$ can be divided into foreground and background pixels. By definition, foreground pixels are pixels that are a part of the object and every other pixel can be considered as a part of the background. In this paper we make the assumption that the foreground pixels, on their own, carry sufficient predictive power for the task of image classification. Additionally, removing background pixels restricts the input space that the adversary can attack, inhibiting its ability to trigger misclassification in the target model.

For an image $x^{(i)} \in \mathbf{X}$ of resolution $m \times n$, let's define a foreground image $x_{FG}^{(i)} = F(x^{(i)})$, where

$$F(x^{(i)}) = \begin{cases} x_{jk}^{(i)} & \text{if } x_{jk}^{(i)} \in S_{FG}^{(i)} \\ 0 & \text{else} \end{cases} \quad j = 1 \ldots m, k = 1 \ldots n$$

where, $S_{FG}^{(i)}$ is the set of foreground pixels for image $x^{(i)}$. We generate $\mathbf{X}_{FG}$ containing foreground images $x_{FG}^{(i)}$ $\forall x^{(i)} \in \mathbf{X}$. Based on the above, we evaluate two class of models: (1) model trained on $\mathbf{X}$, (2) model trained on $\mathbf{X}_{FG}$. For both, we perform Natural (N) and Adversarial (A) training.

We assume access to foreground masks in our experiments. Thus, our work provides an upper bound on the potential benefit that can be provided by foreground attention masks on model robustness, assuming foreground attention masks can be robustly found. There is some potential hope since recent work has shown that adversarial attacks may be successfully detected on segmentation algorithms [16] using statistical tests, potentially providing a basis for a defense.

3.1   Dataset Creation with Foreground Masks

MS-COCO. We pre-process the MS-COCO dataset to make it compatible with the task of image-classification. Particularly, we use the following pre-processing steps:

- We make use of the semantic segmentation masks and object bounding box annotations to generate image, mask, label pairs such that each image contains object(s) of one label only, or in other words, the mask corresponding to an image contains annotations for one object only.
- To deal with objects having overlapping bounding box regions, we explicitly black-out pixels corresponding to the extra objects.
- We adjust the crop dimensions in order to extract square image patches, and resize all the extracted image patches to 32×32.
- Due to high class-imbalance in the resultant dataset, we ignore the person class (over frequent) and short-list top 10 classes from the remaining classes based on the frequency.

Fig. 2. Visualizing examples in the MS-COCO-IC dataset. We display the original image from the MS-COCO dataset, cropped image of object of interest, and the foreground masked image from left to right.

We call this modified MS-COCO dataset as **MS-COCO-IC**. Table 1 shows the statistics for this dataset. The images in this dataset contain $\approx 56\%$ foreground pixels. Figure 2 gives an example of an original image, the cropped image, and the final image that is used for training a classifier.

Table 1. Number of images per class in the train and test set of our MSCOCO-IC dataset.

Class	Number of images	
	Train	Test
Chair	21674	11077
Car	18498	9594
Book	12094	6188
Bottle	10923	5735
Dinning table	10291	5274
Umbrella	6510	3309
Boat	5531	2797
Motorcycle	5340	2703
Sheep	4748	2432
Cow	4391	2162
Total	100000	51271

GTSRB. The German Traffic Sign Recognition Benchmark (GTSRB) is a dataset containing 50,000 color images of 43 different classes of road signs, with high class imbalance. Images in GTSRB model various viewpoints and light conditions. We use a customized segmenter based on the graph cut algorithm to obtain foreground masks. One favorable aspect of GTSRB is that majority of the traffic signs are centrally located in the image, have regular shapes, and usually possess a sharp color in contrast to the background. These features match the assumptions of our customized segmenter. The images in this dataset contain $\approx 25\%$ foreground pixels. We associate the low percentage of foreground pixels to the imperfections of our ad hoc segmenter. Figure 3 gives an example of an image, computed mask by our segmenter, and the final image that is used for training a classifier.

Fig. 3. Visualizing examples in the GTSRB-IC dataset. We display the natural image, foreground mask and the foreground masked image from left to right.

4   Results

For our experiments, we train two set of models: (1) on natural images; (2) on foreground masked image, both naturally and adversarially. For both, we use the VGG-19 classifier. We evaluate these models against a 10-step $\mathbf{L}_\infty$ bounded PGD adversary with step size of $\frac{2}{255}$ and $\epsilon = \frac{8}{255}$. Treating the performance of models trained on $\mathbf{X}$ as a baseline, we calculate potential gains in robustness in the models trained on $\mathbf{X}_{FG}$. We repeat the above experiments for both GTSRB-IC and MS-COCO-IC datasets. Note that in the case of $\mathbf{X}_{FG}$ models, the adversary is only given access to the foreground pixels. We summarize our results in Table 2.

Table 2. Comparing adversarial robustness of models trained on natural images versus foreground masked images. For both datasets. We observe increased robustness against a PGD adversary when the model and the adversary have access to foreground features only.

Data	Training	MSCOCO-IC		GTSRB-IC	
		Natural	PGD	Natural	PGD
$\mathbf{X}$	Natural	79.46%	2.28%	98.04%	18.69%
$\mathbf{X}_{FG}$	Natural	**81.64%**	**3.01%**	98.04%	**38.38%**
$\mathbf{X}$	Adversarial	61.51%	30.80%	89.54%	55.25%
$\mathbf{X}_{FG}$	Adversarial	**72.92%**	**53.62%**	**91.20%**	**64.57%**

MS-COCO-IC. We can observe from the results that both the naturally trained classifiers exhibit comparable vulnerability to PGD adversary. However, in case of the adversarially trained classifiers, natural and adversarial accuracy increases by 11.41% and 22.82% respectively, on using foreground attention masks. This validates our hypothesis that foreground attention has a positive effect on a model's classification performance and robustness.

GTSRB-IC. Similar to the previous set of results, we see that the model adversarially trained using $\mathbf{X}_{FG}$ is more robust to a PGD adversary than a model adversarially trained using $\mathbf{X}$ (+9.32%). Additionally, we see that the model naturally trained on $\mathbf{X}_{FG}$ exhibits considerable improvement in robustness as compared to the model naturally trained on $\mathbf{X}$ (+19.69%).

5   Conclusion

We study the use of foreground attention masks for improving the robustness of deep neural networks against L_∞-bounded PGD attack. We develop two new datasets based on MS-COCO and GTSRB, to examine these effects. Our preliminary results suggest positive effects in using foreground masks for improving adversarial robustness against PGD adversary. For an adversarially trained model on the MS-COCO-IC dataset, foreground attention masks improved adversarial accuracy by 21.8%. For the GTSRB-IC dataset, when adversarially training a model with foreground masked images, we observe a smaller improvement of 1.7% in adversarial accuracy. Initial results are promising however, further work must be done to verify the effect of foreground attention masks on adversarial robustness and to develop an reliable method to extract these foreground masks automatically.

Prior work by Simon-Gabriel *et al.* [12] suggest that our masking technique improves adversarial robustness due to a reduction in the number of input features. Against a first-order adversary (*e.g.*, PGD attack), they establish that the adversarial robustness scales as $1/\sqrt{d}$ where d is the number of input features. Therefore, masking some of the input features should improve adversarial robustness to some degree. For future work, we intend to investigate this relationship further as we believe that the relative importance of a feature for classification may suggest additional robustness. Also, this relationship might help better explain certain trends that we observe in the results. Such work will help better understand the usefulness of foreground masks in context of adversarial robustness against first-order adversaries.

References

1. Arnab, A., Miksik, O., Torr, P.H.: On the robustness of semantic segmentation models to adversarial attacks. In: IEEE Conference on Computer Vision and Pattern Recognition (2018)
2. Athalye, A., Carlini, N., Wagner, D.: Obfuscated gradients give a false sense of security: circumventing defenses to adversarial examples. In: International Conference on Machine Learning (2018)
3. Chen, J., Wu, X., Liang, Y., Jha, S.: Improving adversarial robustness by data-specific discretization. arXiv preprint arXiv:1805.07816 (2018)
4. Chen, L.C., Papandreou, G., Schroff, F., Adam, H.: Rethinking atrous convolution for semantic image segmentation. arXiv preprint arXiv:1706.05587 (2017)
5. Harley, A.W., Derpanis, K.G., Kokkinos, I.: Segmentation-aware convolutional networks using local attention masks. In: International Conference on Computer Vision, October 2017
6. Lamb, A., Binas, J., Goyal, A., Serdyuk, D., Subramanian, S., Mitliagkas, I., Bengio, Y.: Fortified networks: improving the robustness of deep networks by modeling the manifold of hidden representations. arXiv preprint arXiv:1804.02485 (2018)
7. Liao, F., Liang, M., Dong, Y., Pang, T., Zhu, J., Hu, X.: Defense against adversarial attacks using high-level representation guided denoiser. In: IEEE Conference on Computer Vision and Pattern Recognition (2018)
8. Lin, T.-Y., Maire, M., Belongie, S., Hays, J., Perona, P., Ramanan, D., Dollár, P., Zitnick, C.L.: Microsoft COCO: common objects in context. In: Fleet, D., Pajdla, T., Schiele, B., Tuytelaars, T. (eds.) ECCV 2014. LNCS, vol. 8693, pp. 740–755. Springer, Cham (2014). https://doi.org/10.1007/978-3-319-10602-1_48
9. Madry, A., Makelov, A., Schmidt, L., Tsipras, D., Vladu, A.: Towards deep learning models resistant to adversarial attacks. In: International Conference on Learning Representation (2018)

10. Ronneberger, O., Fischer, P., Brox, T.: U-Net: convolutional networks for biomedical image segmentation. In: Navab, N., Hornegger, J., Wells, W.M., Frangi, A.F. (eds.) MICCAI 2015. LNCS, vol. 9351, pp. 234–241. Springer, Cham (2015). https://doi.org/10.1007/978-3-319-24574-4_28

11. Schott, L., Rauber, J., Bethge, M., Brendel, W.: Towards the first adversarially robust neural network model on mnist. arXiv preprint arXiv:1805.09190 (2018)

12. Simon-Gabriel, C.J., Ollivier, Y., Bottou, L., Schölkopf, B., Lopez-Paz, D.: Adversarial vulnerability of neural networks increases with input dimension. arXiv preprint arXiv:1802.01421 (2018)

13. Stallkamp, J., Schlipsing, M., Salmen, J., Igel, C.: Man vs. computer: benchmarking machine learning algorithms for traffic sign recognition. Neural Netw. **32**, 323–332 (2012)

14. Szegedy, C., et al.: Intriguing properties of neural networks. In: International Conference on Learning Representations (2014)

15. Wu, H., Zhang, J., Huang, K., Liang, K., Yu, Y.: FastFCN: rethinking dilated convolution in the backbone for semantic segmentation. arXiv preprint arXiv:1903.11816 (2019)

16. Xiao, C., Deng, R., Li, B., Yu, F., Liu, M., Song, D.: Characterizing adversarial examples based on spatial consistency information for semantic segmentation. In: Ferrari, V., Hebert, M., Sminchisescu, C., Weiss, Y. (eds.) ECCV 2018. LNCS, vol. 11214, pp. 220–237. Springer, Cham (2018). https://doi.org/10.1007/978-3-030-01249-6_14

17. Xie, C., Wu, Y., Maaten, L.v.d., Yuille, A.L., He, K.: Feature denoising for improving adversarial robustness. In: IEEE Conference on Computer Vision and Pattern Recognition (2019)

Learner-Independent Targeted Data Omission Attacks

Guy Barash[1], Onn Shehory[1(✉)], Sarit Kraus[1], and Eitan Farchi[2]

[1] Bar Ilan University, Ramat Gan, Israel
guy.barash@wdc.com, onn.shehory@biu.ac.il, sarit@cs.biu.ac.il
[2] IBM Haifa Research, Haifa, Israel
farchi@il.ibm.com

Abstract. In this paper we introduce the *data omission attack*—a new type of attack against learning mechanisms. The attack can be seen as a specific type of a poisoning attack. However, while poisoning attacks typically corrupt data in various ways including addition, omission and modification, to optimize the attack, we focus on omission only, which is much simpler to implement and analyze. A major advantage of our attack method is its generality. While poisoning attacks are usually optimized for a specific learner and prove ineffective against others, our attack is effective against a variety of learners. We demonstrate this effectiveness via a series of attack experiments against various learning mechanisms. We show that, with a relatively low attack budget, our omission attack succeeds regardless of the target learner.

Keywords: Adversarial ML · Machine learning

Machine learning techniques are widely used for real-world prediction and decision making. Their presence in real systems introduces an array of security risks. However, the vast majority of machine learning mechanisms were not designed with focus on security. This is well recognized by a plethora of studies in the field of adversarial machine learning [20]. Indeed, several attacks on learners have been introduced. Many of these aim to corrupt training data, in order to manipulate the learned model. Attacks of this type are referred to as *poisoning attacks* [7].

In this study we introduce a specific attack—*data omission attack*—that belongs to the family of data poisoning attacks. However, while data poisoning typically requires that the attacker gain access to the learning dataset to modify it, data omission does not necessarily require that. A data omission attack does not modify data points—it merely omits some. Such omission can be performed, e.g., by preventing the addition of some new data points to the dataset. This can be achieved in various ways, e.g., man-in-the-middle, even without direct access to the dataset.

Poisoning attacks typically aim to corrupt the model and impact performance and accuracy. Specifically, they aim at misclassification such that some datapoints, not necessarily specific ones, are erroneously classified. In this study the

O. Shehory et al. (Eds.): EDSMLS 2020, CCIS 1272, pp. 23–41, 2020.
https://doi.org/10.1007/978-3-030-62144-5_3

goal of the attack is different. That is, the goal is to misclassify a specific targeted data-point, and only that specific point, while keeping the accuracy of the model unchanged. We refer to this data omission attack as *Single Point Targeted* attack (SPT attack in short). To our best understanding, no prior study has examined data omission SPT attacks. Recent surveys on poisoning attacks ([7] and [15]) suggest that targeted misclassification attacks are possible. In difference from SPT, those attacks are not necessarily focused on a single data-point. Indeed, those surveys do not identify studies in which single data-point targeted attacks, similar to SPT, are discussed.

Attacks against learning mechanisms, and in particular poisoning attacks, are often designed, applied and evaluated against a specic target learning mechanism. Thus, if an attack proves effective against learner L_1, it may be ineffective against learner L_2. To defend against such attacks, one can allow switching between two or more learners, such that at least one of them is not sensitive to the attack.

In contrast to poisoning attacks in the art, our attack is not specific to a single learner. Rather, it effectively succeeds in attacking a variety of learners. In similarity to earlier studies, we assume that the attacker knows what type of learner it attacks. However, in difference from those, the learner type is merely an input. In response to this input, the attack is optimized to the specific learner. As we demonstrate experimentally, our attack performs well against an array of different learners. Thus, defense via learner switching is inapplicable.

An important property of SPT is its focus on data omission. It is thus much simpler, as there is no need to gain access to the dataset, nor to design and implement data corruption. The latter is a major concern of multiple poisoning attacks. We experimentally demonstrate that, even when relying on omission only, attacks are very effective. We experiment with several different attack methods against several learners to identify the methods that are most effective across learners.

Contribution. The contribution of our study is fourfold. Firstly, we introduce a new, special attack against learners—the data omission attack. Secondly, our attack is effective against a broad class of learners and not just against one specific learner. Thirdly, our attack targets a specific data-point and successfully misclassifies it without affecting the performance of the model overall. Fourthly, the number of points that must be omitted to mount an effective attack (i.e., the budget) is rather small.

1   Related Work

In recent years, security of machine learning mechanisms, including attacks and defenses thereof, has attracted much community attention. Extensive background can be found in, e.g., [3] and [2]. Surveys on relevant taxonomy, and other studies, can be found in [7] and [5]. This paper, too, discusses security issues of machine learning mechanisms, focusing on the *data omission SPT attack*.

The data omission attack method we present resembles other attack methods known in the art, however it has some unique differentiating properties. Specifically, since our attack interferes with input data, it is a specific type of a *data poisoning attack*. Poisoning attack methods exhibit several attack approaches, usually adding new data or corrupting existing data (or both). Examples of injecting corrupted data can be found e.g., in [9,21] and [17]. In difference from these, our attack does not involve data injection or corruption – it merely entails data omission. Work in [24] presents a method of modeling attacks against machine learning. It additionally provides metrics by which such attacks can be evaluated and compared. Those metrics examine several capabilities employed by the attack methods of interest, however they do not examine data omission. This further emphasizes the novelty of our method.

Another form of data poisoning is in [27], where no new data is added, but instead labels are changed maliciously. Some poisoning attacks allow data omission, but not as an exclusive element of the attack. For example, in [16], data deletion is suggested as one element of its data manipulation attack. However, that work does not explicitly study the effects of data deletion. In contrast, we focus on exclusive data omission as a major attack vehicle. Attacks in which a single data sample is attacked, resembling the idea of SPT, are in [25] and [6]. There, the sample itself is manipulated with adversarial noise. The SPT method does not modify the attacked sample. Rather, via omission of other samples, the model itself misclassifies the attack sample.

An advantage of using our method stems not from what it does, but from what is **doesn't** do. Classic poisoning attacks, as mentioned above, are known in the art for quite some time. Consequently, several defense methods were developed, e.g., data sanitation [23], [11] and [8]. The attack presented in our study introduces no new data or changed data. Thus, data sanitation cannot defend against it.

Another key difference between this work and other data poisoning, e.g., [4] and [18], is that in previous work the attacker aims to decrease the accuracy of the model, while here attacks target a specific data sample, yet keeping the model's accuracy intact for other test samples.

While effective, the poisoning attacks mentioned above and others such as [10, 13], [19] and [11] each targets a specific learner. The attack method we suggest does not target a specific learner. Rather, it can be applied to a variety of learners. Given a learner type as input, it adapts to that specific learner to perform an omission attack on it. To our best understanding, no other poisoning attack exhibits this cross-learner capability.

2   Problem and Solution Approach

We refer to a general classification learning setting. We assume a dataset $S = \{s_i | 1 \leq i \leq N\}, \forall i. s_i \in \mathbb{R}^N$. We additionally assume c classes, whose labels are $LB = \{l_1, l_2, \ldots, l_c\}$. Each $s_i \in S$ belongs to one of these classes. Given the dataset S described above, we further assume a learning algorithm L that, given the dataset as input, generates a model $M(S, L)$ that expresses the learned association between data items and class labels.

2.1 Formalization of the Problem

We assume an attacker A that can get the same dataset S as input; the attacker additionally gets a data item s_a for which L learns a specific label $l \in LB$, however A would like to attack the learning such that the learned label will be $\bar{l} \neq l, \bar{l} \in LB \setminus \{l\}$, instead of l. The attacker has an attack budget k. In our case, this budget is the number of data-points A may remove from the dataset. The attacker's capabilities are to strategically select a subset $S_k \subseteq S$ of size no more then $k, |S_k| \leq k$ to remove in order to create a new subset $\hat{S}$ such that $\hat{S} \cap S_k = \emptyset$ and $\hat{S} \cup S_k = S$.

The attacker's goal is that the model $\hat{M}(\hat{S}, L)$ derived when L is trained on $\hat{S}$ will consistently misclassify s_a, however its accuracy in classifying the other samples will be equivalent to the accuracy delivered by model $M(S, L)$. Here equivalent accuracy entails that the difference between the two accuracies is at most 5%. Recall that we only allow omissions of data points to generate $\hat{S}$. Our goal is to develop methods for an attacker to successfully preform such attacks.

2.2 Methodology and Experimental Environment

The attack methods we suggest to address the above problem each implements a specific strategy for selecting the points to be omitted from the dataset. This strategy is the essence of each attack method. We specifically introduce three attack methods: KNN, Greedy and Genetic, of which details are presented in Sect. 3. In this study we show that the suggested attack methods indeed provide the sought result, i.e., misclassification of s_a. This is performed via an array of experiments, applied to two different datasets.

The experiments we perform are comprised of multiple iterations. An experiment's iteration i refers to a specific dataset S_i, a specific learner L_i, a specific attack method A_i, a specific attack budget k_i, and a specific target data-point to be attacked $s_a{}^i$. Within an experiment, across iterations, some of these elements may vary to meet experimental goals (e.g., the attack budget, or the method, may vary). The flow of an experimental iteration i is as follows:

1. Pre-attack stage
   (a) Employ learner L_i to build a model $M_i(S_i, L_i)$.
   (b) Use $M_i(S_i, L_i)$ to predict the class of $s_a{}^i$, to make sure the model works. In case the model misclassifies $s_a{}^i$ prior to the attack we re-select $s_a{}^i$.
   (c) Measure the accuracy Ac of $M_i(S_i, L_i)$ on a random dataset drawn from the same distribution as S_i.
2. Attack and post-attack stage
   (a) Apply Attack A_i on S_i to create a new, reduced dataset $\hat{S}_i$.
   (b) Employ L_i to build a model $\hat{M}_i(\hat{S}_i, L_i)$.

(c) Use $\hat{M}_i(\hat{S}_i, L_i)$ to predict the class of $s_a{}^i$, to examine the success of the attack.

(d) Measure accuracy $\widehat{Ac}$ of $\hat{M}_i(\hat{S}_i, L_i)$. If $Ac - \widehat{Ac} > 5\%$ report accuracy drop.

In the first set of experiments (*Set I*), our goal is to examine the success and the effectiveness of the attacks, and the vulnerability of the learners, across learner types and attack methods. We thus perform multiple experiments to allow examination of multiple attack-learner combinations. We repeat each experiment several times to validate and increase confidence. The large number of experiments needed in this set imposed a performance constraint. To enable completion in acceptable time, we had to make sure that the dataset is not too large and complex, yet allows for meaningful learning. To this end, we generated a dataset (*Dataset I*), similar to the dataset used in [4] in which data points are in $\mathbb{R}^2$, and $c = 2$ (that is, we have two classes—*Blue* and *Red*). This is sufficient for the goals of *Set I*. It is additionally very convenient for visualizing the learning and the attacks, as we demonstrate later.

In the second set of experiments (*Set II*), the attack will be preformed on the MNIST [12] dataset. This should provide a more realistic, widely used learning environment ([22] and [28] for example). The dimensionality of samples in MNIST, and the number of classes thereof, is significantly larger than the number of those in *Dataset I*. As a result, the computation required for executing an exhaustive experiment as done for *Set I* is prohibitively large. To mitigate this problem, in *Set II* we will experiment with only one attack method and one learner. Specifically, the attacker that will prove the most successful in *Set I* and the learner that will be the most difficult to manipulate in *Set I*, will be used in *Set II*. This choice aims to examine our best attack method against the most challenging learner. Examining weaker attack methods is not as important, as we assume that, if the best attacker fails, others will fail as well. Similarly, examining less challenging learners is not as important, as we assume that, if an attack on the most robust learner succeeds, it will succeed against weaker learners as well.

Experiment *Set I:* attack on *Dataset I*. In experiment Set I we will examine the attack methods we have devised and their success. We will do this in various environments and parameter values, e.g., different learners, different attack budgets, etc. Each experiment in this set entails a coupling between an attack method A and a learning algorithm L, aiming to examine the success of A in attacking L. Each such experiment comprises multiple iterations, where the attack budget k and difficulty level D, as will be defined below, are varied across iterations. Each such iteration (keeping $A, L, k,$ and D fixed) may be repeated several times to study stability.

An iteration in *Set I* consists of the following elements: a dataset S, a budget k, a difficulty parameter D that determines the position of the data sample to be attacked s_a (denoted attack point), an attack method A, and a learner L. The dataset S comprises 400 data samples, generated from a 2-dimensional normal distribution. 200 samples are generated with a center-point c_r, and labeled

$l = RED$. Additional 200 samples are generated from a similar distribution but with a different center-point c_b, and labeled $l = BLUE$.

Once S is populated, the attack point s_a is determined. The goal is for s_a to be placed such that, geometrically, it is well within the RED class, so that misclassification is not trivial. A successful attack should result in the learner misclassifying s_a as $BLUE$ instead of RED. To generate such a placement, the following procedure is performed (see Fig. 1 for a graphical illustration). A straight line l_n will be drawn between the data distribution centers, from c_r to c_b. To make sure the attack point is more likely to be RED prior to the attack, a point p_r is marked on l_n which is closer to c_r at a ratio of $7 : 10$.[1] A line l_p, perpendicular to l_n is drawn, crossing l_n at point p_r. The attack point s_a will be placed on l_p. Via multiple experiments we have learned that, the closer s_a (on line l_p) is to l_n—the harder it is to successfully attack and misclassify it. To examine various levels of difficulty in misclassification, the distance of s_a from l_n will be varied across experiment iterations. This is expressed by the distance parameter D, also referred to as difficulty parameter or value. When $D = 0$, s_a is on l_n, and when $D = 25$, s_a is 25 units of distance from l_n. Notice that, as D increases, the difficulty of misclassifying s_a decreases. The distance is illustrated in Fig. 1.

Once parameters are set, the iteration can proceeds to the attack phase. Then, given k, the attacker determines the optimal k points to remove from S, and returns $S_k \subseteq S, |S_k| = k$, the "attacked" dataset, which is identical to S except for k omitted points. As stated above, each experiment in $Set\ I$ focuses on a specific attack method $A \in \{KNN, Greedy, Genetic\}$ and a specific learner $L \in \{NeuralNetwork, RandomForest, KNN, SVM\}$. Experimenting with multiple learning methods serves for proving the broad applicability of our attack method. Within the experiment, across iterations, parameters are varied, i.e., each iteration has a specific budget $k \in 1, \ldots, 20$ and a specific difficulty $D \in 1, \ldots, 25$. As suggested, an iteration is repeated at least 20 times, to show stability.

The success of an attack is measured via the prediction probability of model $M(S, L)$ when attempting to classify point s_a as RED, denoted as - $PR(L, S, RED, s_a) \in [0, 1]$. An attack is considered successful if - $PR(L, S, RED, s_a) \geq 0.5$ and $PR(L, \hat{S}, RED, s_a) < 0.5$. This means that the attacked model has misclassified s_a. While a success of our attack method changes the label of s_a, the accuracy of the model is not affected. That is, the accuracy of $\hat{M}(\hat{S}, L)$ is equivalent to the accuracy of $M(S, L)$.

Experiment $Set\ II$: attack on MNIST. In this experiment set, the MNIST dataset is used. MNIST is a realistic dataset that is widely used for machine learning experiments. It contains figures of handwritten digits, each figure is 28×28 pixels in gray-scale. The digit figures in MNIST are labeled, where a label is the digit that appears in the corresponding figure (i.e., labels are

---

[1] Any ratio that results in p_r being closer to c_r than to c_b should work. However, following a set of experiments we concluded that the 7:10 ratio provides a nontrivial attack challenge, thus facilitating the goal of our study.

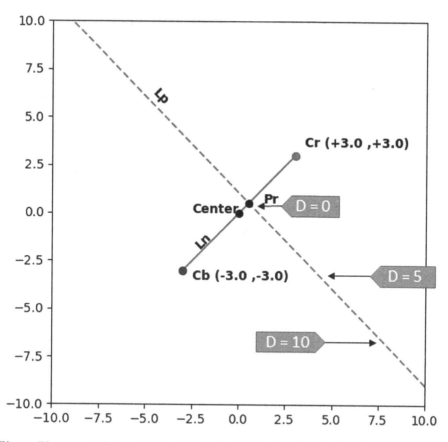

Fig. 1. Placement of the attack point s_a in *Set I*: the point is placed on the l_p line. Various locations (expressed by D values) on that line are examined to study diverse attack difficulty levels.

$\in \{0, 1, \ldots, , 9\}$). In this experiment, the goal of our attack is, given a new digit figure whose correct label is l, and given label $\hat{l}$, to cause the learner to predict $\hat{l}$ instead of l. To examine our attack method, we construct 90 datasets by sampling MNIST, where each dataset comprises 201 samples: a 101 samples of one digit d and 100 samples of another digit $d' \neq d$. Given 10 different digit labels, there are 45 possible label pairs. Since order within the pair is important, we have 90 ordered pairs of labels. For each such pair we construct one dataset, as described above. In the experiment, our attack is applied to each and every such dataset. To generalize the attack, and for uniformity with the previous experiment, we annotate a 100 d samples as *RED* and a 100 d' samples as *BLUE*. An additional d sample serves as the target data-point to be attacked. The dataset comprising the two sets of size 100 is denoted as $S^{<R,B>}$ and the adversarial sample is denoted as $s_a^{<R,B>}$. The 201 samples are drawn randomly from the MNIST dataset (Fig. 2).

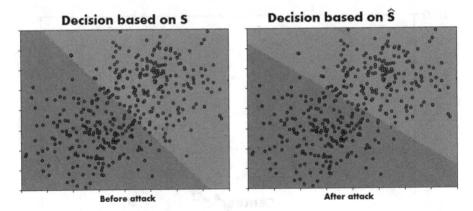

Fig. 2. Example before and after a successful attack. s_a is marked as a yellow square. Budget $k = 13$

Note that, as a result of the exhaustive study of label pairs, within this experiment, we must perform many more experiment instances compared to experiment *Set I*. Thus, to minimize execution time, in *Set II* only one attack method and only one learner are used. The attack method to be selected is the best method (in terms of success rate) identified in *Set I*. The learner to be selected is the one that proves most difficult to attack in terms of the budget required for an attack to succeed. The attack point and the specific dataset are changed per iteration and are both drawn from the 90 datasets created as described above.

For each dataset $S^{<R,B>}$ selected we follow the flow in Sect. 2.2. We test each model on the attack point as described in (1) *Pre–attack*, followed by examining the success rate of the attack as described in (2) *Attack and post–attack*. If the success rate is above 0.5 the attack is considered a success. To ensure stability of the results, the flow described above is repeated several times for each $S^{<R,B>}$. The results presented are averages over these repetitions.

3 Attack Methods

We describe here the attack methods implemented in this study. The major role of these methods is to determine which data-points should be omitted from the dataset to deliver successful misclassification of the attack point.

3.1 The KNN Attack

The *KNN* (K-nearest-neighbours) attack method is inspired by the KNN classification algorithm [1]. It is deterministic in the way it selects data-points to be omitted. Hence, it is rather simple to implement and experiment with.

INPUT
Budget k;
Attack point s_a;
dataset S;
Learning algorithm L;
OUTPUT
Attacked dataset $\hat{S}$;
ALGORITHM 1
$S_k = \{\}$;
$S_{original} = S$;
for j **in** *(1,..,k)* **do**

> \# Check only points labeled RED
> $S_{red} = \{s_i | label(s_i \in S) = RED\}$;
>
> \# Choose closest red point to attack point
> $s_j = argmin_{s \in S_{red}} d(s_a, s)$
>
> \# Remove it from dataset
> $S_k.append(s_j)$;
> $S.pop(s_j)$;

end
$\hat{S} = S_{original} \setminus S_K$;
Return $\hat{S}$;

Algorithm 1: The KNN attack method

Given a data set $S = s_1, ..s_n$, an attack budget k and an attack point s_a, we calculate the Euclidean distance between each point $s_i, label(s_i) = RED$ and s_a. We choose the k points that are closest to s_a as subset S_k to be removed from S, thus creating the attacked dataset $\hat{S} \doteq S \setminus S_k$. This is described in Algorithm 1.

3.2   The Greedy Attack

The *greedy* attack method, as the name suggests, uses a greedy strategy to determine S_k. Given a dataset S, a budget k, an attack point s_a and a learning algorithm L, the algorithm populates S_k with k points. Each of the points to be included in S_k is computed as follows. We iterate over all of the points $s_i \in S$. In each iteration i we generate $S_i = S \setminus \{s_i\}$ and compute a model $M_i(S_i, L)$. For each i, we use M_i to compute the probability that the label of s_a is RED. We choose the point s_j for which the lowest probability was derived, remove it from S, and add it to S_k. This computation is repeated k times to derive the k points that constitute S_k. This is described in Algorithm 2.

INPUT
Budget k;
Attack point s_a;
dataset S;
Learning algorithm L;
OUTPUT
Attacked dataset $\hat{S}$;
ALGORITHM 2
$S_k = \{\}$;
$S_{original} = S$;
for j **in** $(1,..,k)$ **do**

> \# Greedily Choose the optimal next point
> $s_j = argmin_{s_i \in S}\big(PR(L, S/\{s_i\}, RED, s_a)\big)$
> \# Remove it from dataset
> $S_k.append(s_j)$;
> $S.pop(s_j)$;

end
$\hat{S} = S_{original} \setminus S_K$;
Return $\hat{S}$;

Algorithm 2: The Greedy attack method

3.3   The Genetic Attack

The *genetic* attack method, as the name suggests, uses a genetic optimization algorithm to find the optimal $\hat{S} \doteq S \setminus S_k$ for a successful attack. As commonly done in genetic algorithms, some algorithm parameters are preset or provided as input. In our case, this include the *GEN* and *OS* parameters. The former indicates the number of generations to run, and latter sets the number of off-springs per generation. These two parameters should be set such that they do not prevent convergence. In the context of our algorithm, an offspring is a set $P \subset S$ of size k points, generated via some genetic computation from parent sets. During the genetic process, the quality of each offspring P is evaluated via a fitness function $F(P)$. The offsprings with the highest fitness value will be selected for proceeding generations, and eventually the most fit offspring will be selected as S_k for our attack. The fitness function is defined as follows:

$$F(P) = PR(L, P, BLUE, s_a) \in [0, 1] \tag{1}$$

We initialize the algorithm by creating two k–*combinations* (i.e., two randomly generated subsets of S) $P_1 \subset S$ and $P_2 \subset S$, of potential candidates to populate S_k. Each subset includes k elements, i.e., $|P_1| = |P_2| = k$. P_1, P_2 are the "parents" of the first round of the genetic process. In each generation we first create the offsprings by randomly picking k points from $P_1 \cup P_2$. Each of these offsprings goes through a mutation round, in which each point has a probability $\frac{1}{k}$ of being replaced by another point selected randomly from S. This step is important to avoid local minima. In each generation we measure the fitness (using the fitness function $F()$ described above) of each offspring and each parent. The two offsprings (or parents) that score highest become the parents for the next generation. After the final generation is completed, the top offspring, P_1, is selected as S_k. This is described in Algorithm 3. Note that, in the algorithm, the annotation $Tr(p)$ is a function that equals $TRUE$ with probability p.

INPUT
GEN the number of generations to run;
OS the number of offsprings per generation;
ALGORITHM 3
\# Original parents
$P_1 = k\text{–}combination$ of S;
$P_2 = k\text{–}combination$ of S;
for $g \in (1, .., GEN)$ **do**
    \# Create offsprings
    for $t \in (3, .., OS + 2)$ **do**
        $P_t = k\text{–}combination$ of $(P_1 \cup P_2)$;
    end
    \# Mutate offsprings
    for $t \in (3, .., OS + 2)$ **do**
        $c = 0$;
        for $s \in P_t$ **do**
            if $Tr(\frac{1}{k})$ **then**
                $P_t.pop(s)$;
                c += 1;
            end
        end
        $P_t = P_t \cup c\text{–}combination$ of S;
    end
    \# Choose top-2 runners as new parents
    $\hat{P}_1 = argmax_{P_t} F(S \setminus P_t)$;
    $\hat{P}_2 = argmax_{P_t \neq \hat{P}_1} F(S \setminus P_t)$;
    $P_1 = \hat{P}_1$;
    $P_2 = \hat{P}_2$;
end
\# Pick the current top runner
$S_k = P_1$;
$\hat{S} = S \setminus S_K$;
$Return\ \hat{S}$;

Algorithm 3: Genetic attack method

4   Results and Comparison

In this section, we discuss the results of the experiments. Subsects. 4.1 and 4.2 cover the results of the first experiment set. In Subsect. 4.1 we discuss analysis and comparison among attack methods. In Subsect. 4.2 we discuss comparison among learners. Then, the results of the second experiment set are presented in Subsect. 4.3.

4.1 Analysis and Comparison of Attack Methods

In this section we discuss details of, and comparison among, the three attack methods presented earlier: KNN, Greedy and Genetic. We will use two performance metrics for the comparison. The first metric is the budget required for an attack to succeed. We will study the average budget required for each attack method to become effective; we do that at a variety of *difficulty* levels (D). The second metric is a slightly modified Mean Square Error (MSE), as will be defined later in this section. This metric serves for comparing methods' stability. Here, stability of an attack method L means that the budget required for L to succeed will not exceed the expected budget (as expressed by the trend-line of the success of L as a function of D).

Figure 3 presents the budget required for an attack to succeed (the Y-axis) against the difficulty (the X-axis), comparing the 3 attack methods. For each attack method A the figure presents a success budget line Sb_A, comprised of (up to) 25 points, each corresponding to a difficulty level in the range [25..1] and an attack success budget in the range [1..21]. As suggested in Sect. 2.2, lower values of the difficulty parameter D indicate higher difficulties for an attack to succeed, and vise versa. The Y-axis shows the average budget required to mount a successful attack. For each attack, a budget of up to 20 (omission) points was allowed. Cases in which the attack did not succeed within that budget were considered a failed attack and a default budget of 21 was registered.

Figure 3 shows that the genetic attack is the most effective method. It succeeds in attacking the model at all D values, while both the KNN and the greedy attack methods succeed only for $D \geq 5$. We also observe that in most cases the genetic attack consistently needs the lowest budget to succeed at the same difficulty level. On the other hand, the KNN and the Greedy success budget lines, Sb_{KNN} and Sb_{Greedy}, cross each other, and therefore we cannot say that one attack method is superior to the other.

The methods' stability is compared too. Given an attack method A, its stability is measured using a slightly modified Mean Squared Error ($\widehat{MSE}$). As mentioned before, each point in Fig. 3 is an average over 20 iterations, all with the same learner, attack method and difficulty level. The $\widehat{MSE}$ is computed across these 20 iterations, based on the difference between the budget required for each iteration to succeed in the attack, and the trend-line that fits Sb_A. Notice that we are only interested in cases where we exceed the expected budget. To this end, we slightly modify MSE to set to 0 cases in which the attack method succeeded at a budget smaller than the trend-line budget level, as seen in Eq. 2:

$$\widehat{MSE} = \frac{1}{n}\Sigma_{i=1}^{n}\left(max(0, Y - \hat{Y})\right)^2 \tag{2}$$

The $\widehat{MSE}$ values computed for the three attack method are presented in the following table:

	Genetic	Greedy	KNN
$\widehat{MSE}$	0.39	0.58	0.72

The genetic method has the lowest $\widehat{MSE}$ value and thus is the most stable attack method. The KNN method has the highest $\widehat{MSE}$ value and is thus the least stable method. The $\widehat{MSE}$ results presented here were derived for the three attack methods when applied to $L = SVM$. We have additionally performed similar stability analyses for all of the learners studied in this research (i.e., $L \in \{SVM, ANN, KNN, RandomForest\}$). The $\widehat{MSE}$ values for those learners were very similar to those yielded for $L = SVM$, thus providing no additional insights. For brevity, we do not present these results in the paper.

We can conclude that the Genetic attack method typically needs lower budget in order to succeed in an attack. It is additionally more stable than the other two attack methods.

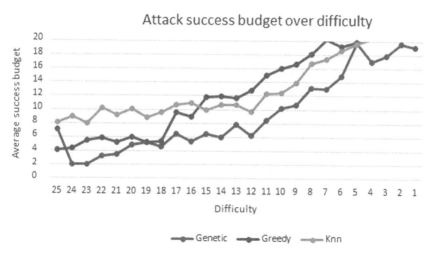

Fig. 3. Comparison between the budgets needed for a successful attack. (Genetic: blue, Greedy: red, KNN: green)

4.2 Attack on Various Learners

To demonstrate the broad applicability of the data omission SPT attack across learners, we have repeated the flow as described in 2.2 with 4 different learners, as follows:

- **ANN:** An Artificial Neural Network (ANN) with 2 hidden layers, each layer with 8 nodes and a Rectified Linear Unit (ReLU) activation function.
- **KNN:** A K-Nearest Neighbor (KNN) classifier, $K = 5$.
- **RandomForest** A RandomForest classifier with 10 trees in the forest.
- **Naive Bayes classifier:** A Gaussian naive Bayes classifier.

As demonstrated in Sects. 3.3 and 4.1, the most cost-effective omission attack method, in most cases, is the *Genetic* attack method. We have therefore applied the genetic omission attack against the four learners. Following, we present the results of this attack on the learners.

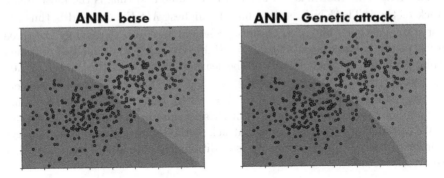

Fig. 4. ANN Model decision line before and after attack

Figure 4 presents the result of an attack against the ANN learner. The border line between blue and red indicates the model's decision line. Each new point introduced to the model to the left of this line will be predicted as Label = $BLUE$ and each new point introduced to the right of that line will be predicted as Label = RED by that model. The image on the left in Fig. 4 visualizes the base decision line, prior to the attack. The image on the right visualizes the post-attack decision line. The point marked by a yellow square is the attack point s_a. As a result of the attack, the decision line has shifted enough to alter the prediction of s_a. Yet, the change in model accuracy was minimal, lesser than 5%, indicating that the attack has introduced a very minor, likely undetectable, change to the model. Consequently, the vast majority of samples were not affected. This desirable property was observed in almost all of the attack experiments we have performed, regardless of attack methods, learners and datasets.

Figures 5, 6 and 7 present the results of attacks (of the Genetic attack method) against the KNN, Naive Bayes and Random Forest learners, respectively. The interpretations of these Figures are similar to the case of attack against ANN shown in Fig. 4. We thus refer here to the difference in results among learners. The attack against KNN, shown in Fig. 5, removed RED points that are close to s_a. The attack against Naive Bayes, shown in Fig. 6, removed RED points that were further from the center of the red cluster than s_a is. The attack against Random Forest, shown in Fig. 7, removed RED points that were to the right of s_a. Regardless of the specific omission strategy, in all cases, the attack was successful within the budget. The change in accuracy as a result of the attack on these learners was similar to the case of ANN. That is, for all learners, the change in model accuracy was minimal, lesser than 5%. As before, this indicates that the attack has introduce a very minor change to the model.

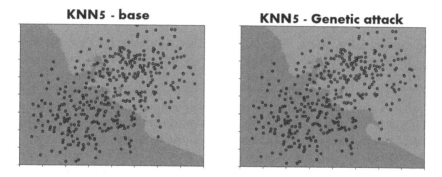

Fig. 5. KNN Model decision line before and after attack

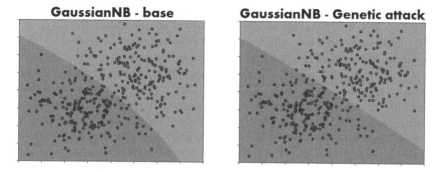

Fig. 6. Naive Bayes Model decision line before and after attack

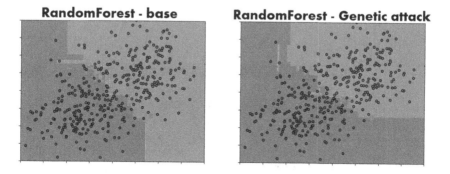

Fig. 7. Random Forest Model decision line before and after attack

In similarity to many learning models, it is not always easy to understand how the genetic attack method chooses its strategy. Nevertheless, it adaptively adjusts to the specific learning model it attacks, and therefore succeeds so well against all learners.

4.3   Attack on MNIST Experiment Analysis

In experiment *Set I*, the *genetic* attack method consistently needs the lowest budget to succeed. Hence, this method was selected for use in experiment *set II*. In *Set I* we also found that *SVM* is the learning algorithm that was the most difficult to attack, in terms of budget required for a successful attack. Therefore, *SVM* was selected as the learner for *Set II*. Figure 8 contains a visualization and comparison of the results. Except for very few cases, the attack is consistently successful. That is, over 92% of the attacks are successful.

Figure 8 indicates attacks that aim to misclassify the digit "1" arrive at lower average success rates. We do not know what the reason for this lower level is. We can speculate that it is related to unique graphical features of the digit "1". For example, "1" is a simple straight line, and this may result in difficulty to classify as another, more complex digit. This insight is supported in multiple studies ([14,26]) in which the accuracy of correct prediction of the digit "1" is greater than the accuracy of all other digits' predictions.

In summary, both of the experimental sets we have conducted indicate that the data omission SPT attack succeeds in attacking various learners. We have empirically shown that multiple omission attack strategies prove successful at a rather low attack budget. We have also shown that omission attacks succeed even when datasets differ significantly, by orders of magnitude, in the number of features of their data samples. We have further empirically examined the stability of attack methods, and found out that the genetic method is the most stable one. Stability here implies that, at a specific difficulty level, the attack budget required for an attack to succeed has only minor deviations across repeated attacks.

		TRGT										
		0	1	2	3	4	5	6	7	8	9	AVG
	0		0.52	0.84	0.94	0.84	0.84	0.66	0.86	1.00	0.67	0.80
	1	0.29		0.24	0.74	0.14	0.85	0.46	0.49	0.82	0.36	0.49
	2	0.68	0.90		0.97	0.83	0.89	0.99	0.90	0.96	0.73	0.87
	3	0.77	0.74	0.94		0.86	0.99	0.87	0.93	0.94	0.87	0.88
	4	0.57	0.50	0.77	0.81		0.77	0.58	0.88	0.86	0.95	0.74
SRC	5	0.88	0.84	0.74	0.97	0.99		0.89	0.97	0.94	0.90	0.90
	6	0.83	0.70	0.99	0.75	0.74	0.97		0.67	0.78	0.59	0.78
	7	0.45	0.61	0.68	0.94	0.90	0.91	0.55		0.61	0.92	0.73
	8	0.67	0.86	0.97	0.92	0.79	1.00	0.76	0.87		0.79	0.85
	9	0.64	0.35	0.90	0.99	0.98	0.99	0.66	0.93	0.88		0.81
	AVG	0.64	0.67	0.79	0.89	0.79	0.91	0.71	0.83	0.87	0.75	0.79

Fig. 8. Success in misclassification from the class in the X axis to the class in the Y axis. Darker background indicates a higher success rate in misclassification, and vice versa.

5 Conclusion

We have introduced a novel poisoning attack—the data omission SPT attack. The focus of our attack on data omission only results in an attack that is much simpler to execute, as there is no need to gain access to the dataset, and there is no need to design and implement data corruption. The targeting of a specific single data sample to be misclassified is another novel property of our attack. As shown, we succeed in attacking the targeted point without affecting model accuracy, thus leaving the vast majority of samples in the dataset intact.

We have experimentally demonstrated that attacks that rely on data omission only are very effective. We experimented with several different attack methods against several learners. The results of these experiments clearly show that our attack methods have several advantages that are not present in existing attacks, as detailed below. Firstly, the attacks are effective against an array of learners and are not limited to a specific learner type, unlike other poisoning attacks. Thus, defense via learner switching is inapplicable. Secondly, small attack budgets, typically an order of magnitude smaller than the size of the dataset, are sufficient for the attack to succeed. Thirdly, the attack methods are effective against both simple and complex datasets, where the feature space is large. Finally, stability of the attack methods is measurable, and at least one of the methods we introduced is very stable.

Our attack exposes a vulnerability of machine learning mechanisms. This calls for careful crafting of proper defense mechanisms. In future work, we plan to study such mechanisms. We also plan to examine additional omission attack strategies and apply them against other types of learners as well. Other datasets should also be examined, with focus on textual ones.

References

1. Altman, N.S.: An introduction to kernel and nearest-neighbor nonparametric regression. Am. Stat. **46**(3), 175–185 (1992)
2. Barreno, M., Nelson, B., Joseph, A.D., Tygar, J.D.: The security of machine learning. Mach. Learn. **81**(2), 121–148 (2010). https://doi.org/10.1007/s10994-010-5188-5
3. Barreno, M., Nelson, B., Sears, R., Joseph, A.D., Tygar, J.D.: Can machine learning be secure? In: Proceedings of the 2006 ACM Symposium on Information, Computer and Communications Security, pp. 16–25. ACM (2006)
4. Biggio, B., Nelson, B., Laskov, P.: Support vector machines under adversarial label noise. In: Asian Conference on Machine Learning, pp. 97–112 (2011)
5. Biggio, B., Roli, F.: Wild patterns: ten years after the rise of adversarial machine learning. Pattern Recognit. **84**, 317–331 (2018)
6. Brown, T.B., Mané, D., Roy, A., Abadi, M., Gilmer, J.: Adversarial patch. arXiv preprint arXiv:1712.09665 (2017)
7. Chakraborty, A., Alam, M., Dey, V., Chattopadhyay, A., Mukhopadhyay, D.: Adversarial attacks and defences: a survey. arXiv preprint arXiv:1810.00069 (2018)
8. Cretu, G.F., Stavrou, A., Locasto, M.E., Stolfo, S.J., Keromytis, A.D.: Casting out demons: Sanitizing training data for anomaly sensors. In: 2008 IEEE Symposium on Security and Privacy (sp 2008), pp. 81–95. IEEE (2008)

9. Fogla, P., Sharif, M.I., Perdisci, R., Kolesnikov, O.M., Lee, W.: Polymorphic blending attacks. In: USENIX Security Symposium, pp. 241–256 (2006)
10. Huang, L., Joseph, A.D., Nelson, B., Rubinstein, B.I., Tygar, J.: Adversarial machine learning. In: Proceedings of the 4th ACM Workshop on Security and Artificial Intelligence, pp. 43–58. ACM (2011)
11. Jagielski, M., Oprea, A., Biggio, B., Liu, C., Nita-Rotaru, C., Li, B.: Manipulating machine learning: poisoning attacks and countermeasures for regression learning. In: 2018 IEEE Symposium on Security and Privacy (SP), pp. 19–35. IEEE (2018)
12. LeCun, Y., Cortes, C.: MNIST handwritten digit database (2010). http://yann.lecun.com/exdb/mnist/
13. Li, B., Vorobeychik, Y.: Feature cross-substitution in adversarial classification. In: Advances in Neural Information Processing Systems, pp. 2087–2095 (2014)
14. Li, L., Zhou, M., Wang, E., Carin, L.: Joint dictionary learning and topic modeling for image clustering, pp. 2168–2171, June 2011. https://doi.org/10.1109/ICASSP.2011.5946757
15. Liu, Q., Li, P., Zhao, W., Cai, W., Yu, S., Leung, V.C.: A survey on security threats and defensive techniques of machine learning: a data driven view. IEEE access 6, 12103–12117 (2018)
16. Ma, Y., Zhu, X., Hsu, J.: Data poisoning against differentially-private learners: attacks and defenses. arXiv preprint arXiv:1903.09860 (2019)
17. Mozaffari-Kermani, M., Sur-Kolay, S., Raghunathan, A., Jha, N.K.: Systematic poisoning attacks on and defenses for machine learning in healthcare. IEEE J. Biomed. Health Inform. 19(6), 1893–1905 (2014)
18. Nelson, B., et al.: Exploiting machine learning to subvert your spam filter. LEET 8, 1–9 (2008)
19. Papernot, N., McDaniel, P., Goodfellow, I.: Transferability in machine learning: from phenomena to black-box attacks using adversarial samples. arXiv preprint arXiv:1605.07277 (2016)
20. Papernot, N., McDaniel, P., Jha, S., Fredrikson, M., Celik, Z.B., Swami, A.: The limitations of deep learning in adversarial settings. In: 2016 IEEE European Symposium on Security and Privacy (EuroS&P), pp. 372–387. IEEE (2016)
21. Rubinstein, B.I., et al.: Antidote: understanding and defending against poisoning of anomaly detectors. In: Proceedings of the 9th ACM SIGCOMM Conference on Internet Measurement, pp. 1–14. ACM (2009)
22. Simard, P.Y., Steinkraus, D., Platt, J.C., et al.: Best practices for convolutional neural networks applied to visual document analysis. In: Icdar, vol. 3 (2003)
23. Steinhardt, J., Koh, P.W.W., Liang, P.S.: Certified defenses for data poisoning attacks. In: Advances in Neural Information Processing Systems, pp. 3517–3529 (2017)
24. Suciu, O., Marginean, R., Kaya, Y., Daume III, H., Dumitras, T.: When does machine learning {FAIL}? Generalized transferability for evasion and poisoning attacks. In: 27th {USENIX} Security Symposium ({USENIX} Security 18), pp. 1299–1316 (2018)
25. Szegedy, C., et al.: Intriguing properties of neural networks. arXiv preprint arXiv:1312.6199 (2013)
26. Wu, M., Zhang, Z.: Handwritten digit classification using the MNIST data set. In: Course project CSE802: Pattern Classification & Analysis (2010)

27. Xiao, H., Biggio, B., Nelson, B., Xiao, H., Eckert, C., Roli, F.: Support vector machines under adversarial label contamination. Neurocomputing **160**, 53–62 (2015)
28. Xingjian, S., Chen, Z., Wang, H., Yeung, D.Y., Wong, W.K., Woo, W.c.: Convolutional lSTM network: a machine learning approach for precipitation nowcasting. In: Advances in Neural Information Processing Systems, pp. 802–810 (2015)

Extraction of Complex DNN Models: Real Threat or Boogeyman?

Buse Gul Atli[1]([⊠]), Sebastian Szyller[1], Mika Juuti[2], Samuel Marchal[1,3], and N. Asokan[2]

[1] Aalto University, 02150 Espoo, Finland
{buse.atli,samuel.marchal}@aalto.fi, contact@sebszyller.com
[2] University of Waterloo, Waterloo, ON N2L 3G1, Canada
mika.juuti@kela.fi, asokan@acm.org
[3] F-Secure Corporation, 00180 Helsinki, Finland

Abstract. Recently, machine learning (ML) has introduced advanced solutions to many domains. Since ML models provide business advantage to model owners, protecting intellectual property of ML models has emerged as an important consideration. Confidentiality of ML models can be protected by exposing them to clients only via prediction APIs. However, model extraction attacks can steal the functionality of ML models using the information leaked to clients through the results returned via the API. In this work, we question whether model extraction is a serious threat to complex, real-life ML models. We evaluate the current state-of-the-art model extraction attack (Knockoff nets) against complex models. We reproduce and confirm the results in the original paper. But we also show that the performance of this attack can be limited by several factors, including ML model architecture and the granularity of API response. Furthermore, we introduce a defense based on distinguishing queries used for Knockoff nets from benign queries. Despite the limitations of the Knockoff nets, we show that a more realistic adversary can effectively steal complex ML models and evade known defenses.

Keywords: Machine learning · Model extraction · Deep neural networks

1 Introduction

In recent years, machine learning (ML) has been applied to many areas with impressive results. Use of ML models is now ubiquitous. Major enterprises (Google, Apple, Facebook) utilize them in their products [29]. Companies gain business advantage by collecting proprietary data and training high quality models. Hence, protecting the intellectual property embodied in ML models is necessary to preserve the business advantage of model owners.

Increased adoption of ML models and popularity of centrally hosted services led to the emergence of *Prediction-As-a-Service* platforms. Rather than distributing ML models to users, it is easier to run them on centralized servers having powerful computational resources and to expose them via *prediction APIs*.

© Springer Nature Switzerland AG 2020
O. Shehory et al. (Eds.): EDSMLS 2020, CCIS 1272, pp. 42–57, 2020.
https://doi.org/10.1007/978-3-030-62144-5_4

Prediction APIs are used to protect the confidentiality of ML models and allow for widespread availability of ML-based services that require users only to have an internet connection. Even though users only have access to a prediction API, each response necessarily leaks some information about the model. A *model extraction attack* [31] is one where an adversary (a malicious client) extracts information from a *victim model* by frequently querying the model's prediction API. Queries and API responses are used to build a *surrogate model* with comparable functionality and effectiveness. Deploying surrogate models deprive the model owner of its business advantage. Many extraction attacks are effective against simple ML models [9,24] and defenses have been proposed against these simple attacks [18,25]. However, extraction of complex ML models has got little attention to date. Whether model extraction is a serious and realistic threat to real-life systems remains an open question.

Recently, a novel model extraction attack *Knockoff nets* [22] has been proposed against complex deep neural networks (DNNs). The paper reported empirical evaluations showing that Knockoff nets is effective at stealing *any* image classification model. This attack assumes that the adversary has access to (a) *pre-trained* image classification models that are used as the basis for constructing the surrogate model, (b) unlimited natural samples that are not drawn from the same distribution as the training data of the victim model and (c) the full probability vector as the output of the prediction API. Knockoff nets does not require the adversary to have any knowledge about the victim model, training data or its classification task (class semantics). Although other and more recent model extraction attacks have been proposed [3,8,19], Knockoff nets remains the most effective one against complex DNN models with the weakest adversary model. Moreover, there is no detection mechanism specifically tailored against model extraction attacks leveraging unlabeled natural data. Therefore, the natural question is whether Knockoff nets is a realistic threat through extensive evaluation.

Goals and Contributions. Our goals are twofold in this paper. First, we want to understand the conditions under which Knockoff nets constitutes a realistic threat. Hence, we empirically evaluate the attack under different adversary models. Second, we want to explore whether and under which conditions Knockoff nets can be mitigated or detected. We claim the following contributions:

- reproduce the empirical evaluation of Knockoff nets under its original adversary model to confirm that it can extract surrogate models exhibiting reasonable accuracy (53.5–94.8%) for all five complex victim DNN models we built (Sect. 3.2).
- introduce a defense, within the same adversary model, to detect Knockoff nets by differentiating in- and out-of-distribution queries (attacker's queries). This defense correctly detects up to 99% of adversarial queries (Sect. 4).
- revisit the original adversary model to investigate how the attack effectiveness changes with more realistic adversaries and victims (Sect. 5.1). The attack effectiveness deteriorates when

- the adversary uses a model architecture for the surrogate that is different from that of the victim.
- the granularity of the victim's prediction API output is reduced (returning predicted class instead of a probability vector).
- the diversity of adversary queries is reduced.

On the other hand, the attack effectiveness can increase when the adversary has access to natural samples drawn from the *same* distribution as the victim's training data. In this case, all existing attack detection techniques, including our own, are no longer applicable (Sect. 5.4).

2 Background

2.1 Deep Neural Networks

A DNN is a function $F : \mathbb{R}^n \to \mathbb{R}^m$, where n is the number of input features and m is the number of output classes in a classification task. $F(x)$ gives a vector of length m containing probabilities p_j that input x belongs to each class $c_j \in C$ for $j \in \{1, m\}$. The predicted class, denoted $\hat{F}(x)$, is obtained by applying the *argmax* function: $\hat{F}(x) = argmax(F(x))$. $\hat{F}(x)$ tries to approximate a perfect oracle function $O_f : \mathbb{R}^n \to C$ which gives the true class c for any input $x \in \mathbb{R}^n$. The test accuracy $Acc(F)$ expresses the degree to which F approximates O_f.

2.2 Model Extraction Attacks

In a model extraction attack, the goal of an adversary $\mathcal{A}$ is to build a surrogate model $F_{\mathcal{A}}$ that imitates the model $F_{\mathcal{V}}$ of a victim $\mathcal{V}$. $\mathcal{A}$ wants to find an $F_{\mathcal{A}}$ having $Acc(F_{\mathcal{A}})$ as close as possible to $Acc(F_{\mathcal{V}})$ on a test set. $\mathcal{A}$ builds its own dataset $D_{\mathcal{A}}$ and implements the attack by sending queries to the prediction API of $F_{\mathcal{V}}$ and obtaining predictions $F_{\mathcal{V}}(x)$ for each query x, where $\forall x \in D_{\mathcal{A}}$. $\mathcal{A}$ uses the *transfer set* $\{D_{\mathcal{A}}, F_{\mathcal{V}}(D_{\mathcal{A}})\}$ to train a surrogate model $F_{\mathcal{A}}$.

According to prior work on model extraction [9,24], we can divide $\mathcal{A}$'s capabilities into three categories: *victim model knowledge, data access, querying strategy*.

Victim Model Knowledge. Model extraction attacks operate in a *black-box* setting. $\mathcal{A}$ does not have access to model parameters of $F_{\mathcal{V}}$ but can query the prediction API without any limitation on the number of queries. $\mathcal{A}$ might know the exact architecture of $F_{\mathcal{V}}$, its hyperparameters or its training process. Given the purpose of the API (e.g., image recognition) and expected complexity of the task, $\mathcal{A}$ may attempt to guess the architecture of $F_{\mathcal{V}}$ [24]. $F_{\mathcal{V}}$'s prediction API may return one of the following: the probability vector, top-k labels with confidence scores or only the predicted class.

Data Access. Possible capabilities of $\mathcal{A}$ for data access vary in different model extraction attacks. $\mathcal{A}$ can have access to a small subset of natural samples from $\mathcal{V}$'s training dataset [9,24]. $\mathcal{A}$ may not have access to $\mathcal{V}$'s training dataset $D_{\mathcal{V}}$

but may know the "domain" of data and have access to natural samples that are close to $\mathcal{V}$'s training data distribution (e.g., images of dogs in the task of identifying dog breeds) [3]. $\mathcal{A}$ can use widely available natural samples that are different from $\mathcal{V}$'s training data distribution [22]. Finally, $\mathcal{A}$ can construct $D_{\mathcal{A}}$ with only synthetically crafted samples [31].

Querying Strategy. Querying is the process of submitting a sample to the prediction API. If $\mathcal{A}$ relies on synthetic data, it crafts samples that would help it train $F_{\mathcal{A}}$ iteratively. Otherwise, $\mathcal{A}$ first collects its samples $D_{\mathcal{A}}$, queries the prediction API with the complete $D_{\mathcal{A}}$, and then trains the surrogate model with $\{D_{\mathcal{A}}, F_{\mathcal{V}}(D_{\mathcal{A}})\}$.

3   Knockoff Nets Model Extraction Attack

In this section, we study the Knockoff nets model extraction attack [22] which achieves state-of-the-art performance against complex DNN models. Knockoff nets works without access to $\mathcal{V}$'s training data distribution, model architecture and classification task.

3.1   Attack Description

Adversary Model. The goal of $\mathcal{A}$ is *model functionality stealing* [22]: $\mathcal{A}$ wants to train a surrogate model $F_{\mathcal{A}}$ that performs similarly on a classification task for which prediction API's $F_{\mathcal{V}}$ was designed. $\mathcal{A}$ has no information about $F_{\mathcal{V}}$ including model architecture, internal parameters and hyperparameters. Moreover, $\mathcal{A}$ does not have access to $\mathcal{V}$'s training data, prediction API's purpose or output class semantics. $\mathcal{A}$ is a weaker adversary than previous work in [9, 24] due to these assumptions. However, $\mathcal{A}$ can collect an unlimited amount of varied real-world data from online databases and can query prediction API without any constraint on the number of queries. API always returns a complete probability vector as an output for each legitimate query. $\mathcal{A}$ is not constrained in memory and computational capabilities and uses publicly available pre-trained complex DNN models as a basis for $F_{\mathcal{A}}$ [13].

Attack Strategy. $\mathcal{A}$ first collects natural data from online databases for constructing unlabeled dataset $D_{\mathcal{A}}$. For each query x, $\forall x \in D_{\mathcal{A}}$, $\mathcal{A}$ obtains a complete probability vector $F_{\mathcal{V}}(x)$ from the prediction API. $\mathcal{A}$ uses this transfer set $\{D_{\mathcal{A}}, F_{\mathcal{V}}(D_{\mathcal{A}})\}$ to repurpose learned features of a complex pre-trained model with transfer learning [14]. In the Knockoff nets setting, $\mathcal{V}$ offers image classification and $\mathcal{A}$ constructs $D_{\mathcal{A}}$ by sampling a subset of the ImageNet dataset [4].

3.2   Knockoff Nets: Evaluation

We first implement Knockoff nets under the original adversary model explained in Sect. 3.1. We use the datasets and experimental setup described in [22] for constructing both $F_{\mathcal{V}}$ and $F_{\mathcal{A}}$. We also evaluate two additional datasets to contrast our results with previous work.

Datasets. We use Caltech [5], CUBS [32] and Diabetic Retinopathy (Diabetic5) [10] datasets as in [22] for training F_V's and reproduce experiments where Knockoff nets was successful. Caltech is composed of various images belonging to 256 different categories. CUBS contains images of 200 bird species and is used for fine-grained image classification tasks. Diabetic5 contains high-resolution retina images labeled with five different classes indicating the presence of diabetic retinopathy. We augment Diabetic5 using preprocessing techniques recommended in[1] to address the class imbalance problem. For constructing D_A, we use a subset of ImageNet, which contains 1.2M images belonging to 1000 different categories. D_A includes randomly sampled 100,000 images from Imagenet, 100 images per class. 42% of labels in Caltech and 1% in CUBS are also present in ImageNet. There is no overlap between Diabetic5 and ImageNet labels.

Additionally, we use CIFAR10 [15], depicting animals and vehicles divided into 10 classes, and GTSRB [27], a traffic sign dataset with 43 classes. CIFAR10 contains broad, high level classes while GTSRB contains domain specific and detailed classes. These datasets do not overlap with ImageNet labels and they were partly used in prior model extraction work [9,24]. We resize images with bilinear interpolation, where applicable.

All datasets are divided into training and test sets and summarized in Table 1. All images in both training and test sets are normalized with mean and standard deviation statistics specific to ImageNet.

Table 1. Image datasets used to evaluate Knockoff nets. GTSRB and CIFAR10 are resized with bilinear interpolation before training pre-trained classifiers.

Dataset	Image size	Num. of classes	Number of samples	
			Train	Test
Caltech	224 × 224	256	23,703	6,904
CUBS	224 × 224	200	5994	5794
Diabetic5	224 × 224	5	85,108	21,278
GTSRB	32 × 32/224 × 224	43	39,209	12,630
CIFAR10	32 × 32/224 × 224	10	50,000	10,000

Training Victim Models. To obtain complex victim models, we fine-tune weights of a pre-trained ResNet34 [6] model. We train 5 complex victim models using the datasets summarized in Table 1 and name these victim models {Dataset name}-RN34. In training, we use SGD optimizer with an initial learning rate of 0.1 that is decreased by a factor of 10 every 60 epochs over 200 epochs.

Training Surrogate Models. To build surrogate models, we fine-tune weights of a pre-trained ResNet34 [6] model. We query F_V's prediction API with samples

---

[1] https://github.com/gregwchase/dsi-capstone.

from $D_\mathcal{A}$ and obtain $\{D_\mathcal{A}, F_\mathcal{V}(D_\mathcal{A})\}$. We train surrogate models using an SGD optimizer with an initial learning rate of 0.01 that is decreased by a factor of 10 every 60 epochs over 100 epochs. We use the same model architecture for both $F_\mathcal{V}$ and $F_\mathcal{A}$ in order to replicate the experiments in the original paper. Additionally, we discuss the effect of model architecture mismatch in Sect. 5.1.

Experimental Results. Table 2 presents the test accuracy of $F_\mathcal{V}$ and $F_\mathcal{A}$ in our reproduction as well as experimental results reported in the original paper $(F_{\mathcal{V}_\dagger}, F_{\mathcal{A}_\dagger})$. The attack effectiveness against Caltech-RN34 and CUBS-RN34 models is consistent with the corresponding values reported in [22]. We found that $F_\mathcal{A}$ against Diabetic5-RN34 does not recover the same degree of performance. This inconsistency is a result of different transfer sets labeled by two different $F_\mathcal{V}$'s.

As shown in Table 2, Knockoff nets is effective against pre-trained complex DNN models. Knockoff nets can imitate the functionality of $F_\mathcal{V}$ via $\mathcal{A}$'s transfer set, even though $D_\mathcal{A}$ is completely different from $\mathcal{V}$'s training data. We will discuss the effect of transfer set with more detail in Sect. 5.3.

Table 2. Test accuracy $Acc(\cdot)$ of $F_\mathcal{V}$, $F_\mathcal{A}$ in our reproduction and $F_{\mathcal{V}_\dagger}$, $F_{\mathcal{A}_\dagger}$ reported by [22]. Good surrogate models are in bold based on their performance recovery $(Acc(F_\mathcal{A})/Acc(F_\mathcal{V})\times)$.

$F_\mathcal{V}$	$Acc(F_\mathcal{V})$	$Acc(F_\mathcal{A})$	$Acc(F_{\mathcal{V}_\dagger})$	$Acc(F_{\mathcal{A}_\dagger})$
Caltech-RN34	74.6%	72.2% (**0.97**×)	78.8%	75.4% (**0.96**×)
CUBS-RN34	77.2%	70.9% (0.91×)	76.5%	68.0% (0.89×)
Diabetic5-RN34	71.1%	53.5% (0.75×)	58.1%	47.7% (0.82×)
GTSRB-RN34	98.1%	94.8% (**0.97**×)	–	–
CIFAR10-RN34	94.6%	88.2% (**0.93**×)	–	–

4   Detection of Knockoff Nets Attack

In this section, we present a method designed to detect queries used for Knockoff nets. We analyze attack effectiveness w.r.t. the capacity of the model used for detection and the overlap between $\mathcal{A}$'s and $\mathcal{V}$'s training data distributions. Finally, we investigate attack effectiveness when $\mathcal{A}$'s queries are detected and additional countermeasures are taken.

4.1   Goals and Overview

DNNs are trained using datasets that come from a specific distribution $\mathcal{D}$. Many benchmark datasets display distinct characteristics that make them identifiable (e.g. cars in CIFAR10 vs ImageNet) as opposed to being representative of real-world data [30]. A DNN trained using such data might be overconfident, i.e. it gives wrong predictions with high confidence scores, when it is evaluated with samples drawn from a different distribution $\mathcal{D}'$. Predictive uncertainty is unavoidable when a DNN model is deployed for use via a prediction API. In this case, estimating predictive uncertainty is crucial to reduce over-confidence and provide better generalization for unseen samples. Several methods were introduced [7,17,20] to measure the predictive uncertainty by detecting out-of-distribution samples in the domain of image recognition. Baseline [7] and ODIN [20] methods analyze the softmax probability distribution of the DNN to identify out-of-distribution samples. A recent state-of-the-art-method [17] detects out-of-distribution samples based on their Mahalanobis distance [2] to the closest class-conditional distribution. Although these methods were tested against adversarial samples in evasion attacks, their detection performance against Knockoff nets is unknown. What is more, their performance heavily relies on the choice of threshold value which corresponds to the rate of correctly identified in-distribution samples (TNR rate).

Our goal is to detect queries that do not correspond to the main classification task of $\mathcal{V}$'s model. In case of Knockoff nets, this translates to identifying inputs that come from a different distribution than $\mathcal{V}$'s training set. Queries containing such images constitute the distinctive aspect of the adversary model in Knockoff nets: 1) availability of large amount of unlabeled data 2) limited information about the purpose of the API. To achieve this, we propose a binary classifier based on the ResNet architecture. It differentiates inputs from and out of $\mathcal{V}$'s data distribution. Our binary classifier requires a labeled out-of-distribution dataset for the training phase unlike other detection methods [7,17,20]. However, binary classifiers have higher accuracy in the absence of adversary's queries [1] than one-class classifiers used in the prior work.

Our solution can be used as a filter placed in front of the prediction API.

4.2   Training Setup

Datasets. When evaluating our method, we consider all $F_\mathcal{V}$'s we built before in Sect. 3.2. To train our binary classifiers, we combine $\mathcal{V}$'s training samples that are used to build $F_\mathcal{V}$ (in-distribution) and 90,000 randomly sampled images from ImageNet (out-distribution), 90 images per class. To construct a test dataset, we combine $\mathcal{V}$'s corresponding test samples and another subset of ImageNet containing 10,000 samples, 10 images per class. ImageNet serves the purpose of a varied and easily available dataset that $\mathcal{A}$ could use. We assume that legitimate clients query the prediction API with in-distribution test samples and $\mathcal{A}$ queries it with 10,000 ImageNet samples. In order to measure the generalizability of our detector, we also consider the case where $\mathcal{A}$ queries the prediction API with 20,000 samples from the OpenImages [16] dataset that does not overlap with ImageNet. We use the same test datasets to measure the performance of other state-of-the-art out-of-distribution detectors.

Training Binary Classifer. In our experiments, we examine two types of models: 1) ResNet models trained from scratch and 2) pre-trained ResNet models with frozen weights where we replace the final layer with binary logistic regression. In this section, we refer to different ResNet models as RN followed by the number indicating the number of layers, e.g. RN34; we further use the LR suffix to highlight pre-trained models with a logistic regression layer.

We assign label 0 to in-distribution samples ($\mathcal{V}$'s dataset) and 1 to out-of-distribution samples (90,000 ImageNet samples). All images are normalized according to ImageNet-derived mean and standard deviation. We apply the same labeling and normalization procedure to the $\mathcal{A}$'s transfer sets (both 10,000 ImageNet and 20,000 OpenImages samples). To train models from scratch (models RN18 and RN34), we use the ADAM optimizer [12] with initial learning rate of 0.001 for the first 100 epochs and 0.0005 for the remaining 100 (200 total). Additionally, we repeat the same training procedure while removing images whose class labels overlap with ImageNet from $\mathcal{V}$'s dataset (models RN18*, RN34*, RN18*LR, RN34*LR, RN101*LR, RN152*LR). This will minimize the risk of false positives and simulate the scenario with no overlap between the datasets. To train models with the logistic regression layer (models RN18*LR, RN34*LR, RN101*LR, RN152*LR), we take ResNet models pre-trained on ImageNet. We replace the last layer with a logistic regression model and freeze the remaining layers. We train logistic regression using the LBFGS solver [34] with L2 regularization and use 10-fold cross-validation to find the optimal value of the regularization parameter.

4.3 Experimental Results

We divide our experiments into two phases. In the first phase, we select CUBS and train binary classifiers with different architectures in order to identify the optimal classifier. We assess the results using the rate of correctly detected in-(true negative rate, TNR) and out-of-distribution samples (true positive rate, TPR). In the second phase, we evaluate the performance of the selected optimal architecture using all datasets in Sect. 3.2 and assess it based on the achieved TPR and TNR.

Table 3. Distinguishing $\mathcal{A}$'s ImageNet transfer set (TPR) from in-distribution samples corresponding to CUBS test set (TNR). Results are reported for models trained from scratch (RN18, RN34), trained from scratch excluding overlapping classes (models RN18*, RN34*) and using pre-trained models with logistic regression (models RN18*LR, RN34*LR, RN101*LR, RN152*LR. Best results are in bold.

	Model			
	RN18	RN34	RN18*	RN34*
TPR/TNR	86%/83%	94%/80%	90%/83%	**95%**/82%
	Model			
	RN18*LR	RN34*LR	RN101*LR	RN152*LR
TPR/TNR	84%/84%	93%/89%	93%/**93%**	93%/**93%**

Table 4. Distinguishing in-distribution test samples from $\mathcal{A}$'s transfer set as out-of-distribution samples. Comparison of our method with Baseline [7], ODIN [20] and Mahalanobis [17] w.r.t TPR (correctly detected out-of-distribution samples) and TNR (correctly detected in-distribution samples). Best results are in bold.

$\mathcal{A}$'s transfer set	In-dist. dataset	Ours		Baseline/ODIN/Mahalanobis	
		TPR	TNR	TPR (at TNR Ours)	TPR (at TNR 95%)
ImageNet	Caltech	63%	56%	87%/**88%**/59%	13%/11%/5%
	CUBS	**93%**	**93%**	48%/54%/19%	39%/43%/12%
	Diabetic5	**99%**	**99%**	1% /25%/98%	5%/49%/**99%**
	GTSRB	**99%**	**99%**	42%/56%/71%	77%/94%/89%
	CIFAR10	**96%**	**96%**	28%/54%/89%	33%/60%/91%
OpenImages	Caltech	61%	59%	**83%/83%**/6%	11%/11%/6%
	CUBS	**93%**	**93%**	47%/50%/14%	37%/44%/14%
	Diabetic5	**99%**	**99%**	1%/21%/**99%**	4%/44%/**99%**
	GTSRB	**99%**	**99%**	44%/64%/75%	76%/93%/87%
	CIFAR10	**96%**	**96%**	27%/56%/92%	33%/62%/95%

As presented in the Table 3, we find that the optimal architecture is RN101*LR: pre-trained ResNet101 model with logistic regression replacing the final layer. Table 3 also shows that increasing model capacity improves detection accuracy. For the remaining experiments we use RN101*LR since it achieves the same TPR and TNR as RN152*LR while being faster in inference.

Prior work [14,33] has shown that pre-trained DNN features transfer better when tasks are similar. In our case, half of task is identical to the pre-trained task (recognizing ImageNet images). Thus it might be ideal to avoid modifying network parameters and keep pre-trained model parameters frozen by replacing the last layer with a logistic regression. Another benefit of using logistic regression over complete fine-tuning is that pre-trained embeddings can be *pre-calculated once* at a negligible cost, after which training can proceed without performance penalties on CPU in a matter or minutes. Thus, model owners can cheaply train an effective model extraction defense. Such a defense can have wide applicability for small-scale and medium-scale model owners. Finally, since our defense mechanism is stateless, it does not depend on prior queries made by the adversary nor does it keep other state. It handles each query in isolation; therefore, it can not be circumvented by sybil attacks.

Maintaining high TNR is important for usability reasons. Table 4 showcases results for all datasets. We compare our approach with existing state-of-the-art methods detecting out-of-distribution samples[2] when they are also deployed to identify $\mathcal{A}$'s queries. We report results for these methods with optimal hyperparameters (c.f. Table 4). Note that other methods are threshold-based detectors, they require setting TNR to a value before detecting $\mathcal{A}$'s queries. Our method achieves high TPR (>90%) on all $\mathcal{V}$'s but Caltech-RN34 and very high (>99%)

---

[2] https://github.com/pokaxpoka/deep_Mahalanobis_detector.

for GTSRB-RN34 and Diabetic5-RN34. Furthermore, our method outperforms other state-of-the-art approaches when detecting $\mathcal{A}$'s queries. These results are consistent considering the overlap between $\mathcal{V}$'s training dataset and our subsets of ImageNet and OpenImages ($\mathcal{A}$'s transfer set). GTSRB and Diabetic5 have no overlap with ImageNet or OpenImages. On the other hand, CUBS, CIFAR10 and Caltech contain images that represent either the same classes or families of classes (as in CIFAR10) as ImageNet and OpenImages. This phenomena is particularly pronounced in case of Caltech which has strong similarities to ImageNet and OpenImages. While TPR remains significantly above the random 50%, such a model is not suitable for deployment. Although other methods can achieve higher TPR on Caltech (87–88%), we measured this value with TNR fixed at 56%. All models fail to discriminate Caltech samples from $\mathcal{A}$'s queries when constrained to have a more reasonable TNR 95%. We find that our defense method works better with prediction APIs that have specific tasks (such as traffic sign recognition), as opposed to general purpose classifiers that can classify thousands of fine-grained classes. We will discuss how a more realistic $\mathcal{A}$ can evade these detection mechanisms in Sect. 5.4.

5   Revisiting the Adversary Model

We aim to identify capabilities and limitations of Knockoff nets under different experimental setups with more realistic assumptions. We evaluate Knockoff nets when 1) $F_\mathcal{A}$ ad $F_\mathcal{V}$ have completely different architectures, 2) the granularity of $F_\mathcal{V}$'s prediction API output changes, and 3) $\mathcal{A}$ can access data closer to $\mathcal{V}$'s training data distribution. We also discuss $D_\mathcal{A}$'s effect on the surrogate model performance.

5.1   Victim Model Architecture

We measure the performance of Knockoff nets when $F_\mathcal{V}$ does not use pre-trained DNN model but is trained from scratch with a completely different architecture for its task. We apply 5-layer GTSRB-5L and 9-layer CIFAR10-9L $F_\mathcal{V}$'s as described in previous model extraction work [9]. These models are trained using Adam optimizer with learning rate of 0.001 that is decreased to 0.0005 after 100 epochs over 200 epochs. The training procedure of surrogate models is the same as in Sect. 3.2. Thus, GTSRB-5L and CIFAR10-9L have different architectures and optimization algorithms than those used by $\mathcal{A}$. As shown in Table 5, Knockoff nets performs well when both $F_\mathcal{V}$ and $F_\mathcal{A}$ use pre-trained models even if $\mathcal{A}$ uses a different pre-trained model architecture (VGG16 [26]). However, the attack effectiveness decreases when $F_\mathcal{V}$ is specifically designed for the given task and does not base its performance on any pre-trained model.

5.2   Granularity of Prediction API Output

If $F_\mathcal{V}$'s prediction API gives only the predicted class or truncated results, such as top-k predictions or rounded version of the full probability vector for each query,

Table 5. Test accuracy $Acc(\cdot)$ of $F_\mathcal{V}$, $F_{\mathcal{A}_R}$ and $F_{\mathcal{A}_V}$ and the performance recovery of surrogate models. $\mathcal{A}_R$ uses ResNet34 and $\mathcal{A}_V$ uses VGG16 for surrogate model architecture.

$F_\mathcal{V}$	$Acc(F_\mathcal{V})$	$Acc(F_{\mathcal{A}_R})$	$Acc(F_{\mathcal{A}_V})$
GTSRB-RN34	98.1%	94.8% (0.97×)	90.1 (0.92×)
GTSRB-5L	91.5%	54.5% (0.59×)	56.2 (0.61×)
CIFAR10-RN34	94.6%	88.2% (0.93×)	82.9 (0.87×)
CIFAR10-9L	84.5%	61.4% (0.73×)	64.7 (0.76×)

performance of the surrogate model degrades. Table 6 shows this limitation, where the prediction API gives complete probability vector to $\mathcal{A}_p$ and only predicted class to $\mathcal{A}_c$. Table 6 also demonstrates that the amount of degradation is related to the number of classes in $F_\mathcal{V}$, since $\mathcal{A}$ obtains comparatively less information if the actual number of classes is high and the granularity of response is low. For example, the degradation is severe when Knockoff nets is implemented against Caltech-RN34 and CUBS-RN34 having more than or equal to 200 classes. However, degradation is low or zero when Knockoff nets is implemented against other models (Diabetic5-RN34, GTSRB-RN34, CIFAR10-RN34).

Table 6. Test accuracy $Acc(\cdot)$ of $F_\mathcal{V}$, $F_{\mathcal{A}_p}$, $F_{\mathcal{A}_c}$ and the performance recovery of surrogate models. $\mathcal{A}_p$ receives complete probability vector and $\mathcal{A}_c$ only receives predicted class from the prediction API.

$F_\mathcal{V}$	$Acc(F_\mathcal{V})$	$Acc(F_{\mathcal{A}_p})$	$Acc(F_{\mathcal{A}_c})$
Caltech-RN34 (256 classes)	74.6%	68.5% (0.92×)	41.9% (0.56×)
CUBS-RN34 (200 classes)	77.2%	54.8% (0.71×)	18.0% (0.23×)
Diabetic5-RN34 (5 classes)	71.1%	59.3% (0.83×)	54.7% (0.77×)
GTSRB-RN34 (43 classes)	98.1%	92.4% (0.94×)	91.6% (0.93×)
CIFAR10-RN34 (10 classes)	94.6%	71.1% (0.75×)	53.6% (0.57×)

Many commercial prediction APIs return top-k outputs for queries (Clarifai returns top-10 outputs and Google Cloud Vision returns up to top-20 outputs from more than 10000 labels). Therefore, attack effectiveness will likely degrade when it is implemented against such real-world prediction APIs.

5.3 Transfer Set Construction

When constructing $\{D_\mathcal{A}, F_\mathcal{V}(D_\mathcal{A})\}$, $\mathcal{A}$ might collect images that are irrelevant to the learning task or not close to $\mathcal{V}$'s training data distribution. Moreover, $\mathcal{A}$ might end up having an imbalanced set, where observations for each class are disproportionate. In this case, per-class accuracy of $F_\mathcal{A}$ might be much lower than $F_\mathcal{V}$ for classes with a few observations. Figure 1 shows this phenomenon when $F_\mathcal{V}$ is CIFAR10-RN34. For example, $Acc(F_\mathcal{A})$ is much lower than $Acc(F_\mathcal{V})$ in "deer" and "horse" classes. When the histogram of $\{D_\mathcal{A}, F_\mathcal{V}(D_\mathcal{A})\}$ is checked, the number of queries resulting in these prediction classes are low when compared with other classes. We conjecture that a realistic $\mathcal{A}$ might try to balance the transfer set by adding more observations for underrepresented classes or remove some training samples with less confidence values.

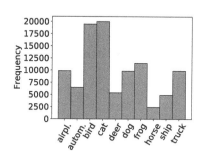

Class name	$Acc(F_\mathcal{V})$	$Acc(F_\mathcal{A})$
Airplane	95%	88% (0.92 ×)
Automobile	97%	95% (0.97 ×)
Bird	92%	87% (0.94 ×)
Cat	89%	86% (0.96 ×)
Deer	95%	84% (**0.88** ×)
Dog	88%	84% (0.95 ×)
Frog	97%	90% (0.92 ×)
Horse	96%	79% (**0.82** ×)
Ship	96%	92% (0.95 ×)
Truck	96%	92% (0.95 ×)

Fig. 1. Histogram of $\mathcal{A}$'s transfer set constructed by querying CIFAR10-RN34 victim model with 100,000 ImageNet samples and per-class test accuracy for victim and surrogate models. The largest differences in per-class accuracies are in bold.

We further investigate the effect of a poorly chosen $D_\mathcal{A}$ by performing Knock-off nets against all $F_\mathcal{V}$'s using Diabetic5 as $D_\mathcal{A}$ (aside from Diabetic5-RN34). We measure $Acc(F_\mathcal{A})$ to be between 3.9–41.9%. The performance degradation in this experiment supports our argument that the $D_\mathcal{A}$ should be chosen carefully by $\mathcal{A}$.

5.4   Access to In-Distribution Data

A realistic $\mathcal{A}$ might know the task of the prediction API and could collect natural samples related to this task. By doing so, $\mathcal{A}$ can improve its surrogate model by constructing $\{D_\mathcal{A}, F_\mathcal{V}(D_\mathcal{A})\}$ that approximates $F_\mathcal{V}$ well without being detected.

In Sect. 4, we observed that the higher the similarity between $\mathcal{A}$'s and $\mathcal{V}$'s training data distribution, the less effective our method becomes. In the worst case, $\mathcal{A}$ has access to a large amount of unlabeled data that does not significantly deviate from $\mathcal{V}$'s training data distribution. In such a scenario, TNR values in Table 4 would clearly drop to 50%. We argue that this limitation is inherent to all detection methods that try to identify out-of-distribution samples.

Publicly available datasets designed for ML research as well as vast databases accessible through search engines and from data vendors (e.g. Quandl, DataSift, Axciom) allow $\mathcal{A}$ to obtain substantial amount of unlabeled data from any domain. Therefore, making assumptions about $\mathcal{A}$'s access to natural data (or lack of thereof) is not realistic. This corresponds to the most capable, and yet plausible, adversary model - one in which $\mathcal{A}$ has approximate knowledge about $\mathcal{V}$'s training data distribution and access to a large, unlabeled dataset. In such a scenario, $\mathcal{A}$'s queries are not going to differ from a benign client, rendering detection techniques ineffective. Therefore we conclude that against a strong, but realistic adversary, the current business model of prediction APIs, which allow a large number of inexpensive queries cannot thwart model extraction attacks.

Even if model extraction attacks can be detected through stateful analysis, highly distributed Sybil attacks are unlikely to be detected. In theory, vendors could charge their customers upfront for a significant number of queries (over 100k), making Sybil attacks cost-ineffective. However, this reduces utility for benign users and restricts the access only to those who can afford to pay. Using authentication for customers or rate-limiting techniques also reduce utility for benign users. Using these methods only slow down the attack and ultimately fail to prevent model extraction attacks.

6   Related Work

There have been several methods proposed to detect or deter model extraction attacks. In certain cases, altering predictions returned to API clients has been shown to significantly deteriorate model extraction attacks: predictions can be restricted to classes [23,31] or adversarially modified to degrade the performance of the surrogate model [18,23]. However, it has been shown that such defenses does not work against all attacks. Model extraction attacks against simple DNNs [9,22,23] are still effective when using only the predicted class. While these defenses may increase the training time of $\mathcal{A}$, they ultimately do not prevent Knockoff nets.

Other works have argued that model extraction defenses alone are not sufficient and additional countermeasures are necessary. In DAWN [28], the authors propose that the victim can poison $\mathcal{A}$'s training process by occasionally returning false predictions, and thus embed a watermark in its model. If $\mathcal{A}$ later makes the surrogate model publicly available for queries, victim can claim ownership using the embedded watermark. DAWN is effective at watermarking surrogate models obtained using Knockoff nets, but requires that $\mathcal{A}$'s model is publicly available for queries and does not protect from the model extraction itself. However, returning false predictions with the purpose of embedding watermarks may be unacceptable in certain deployments, e.g. malware detection. Therefore, accurate detection of model extraction may be seen as a necessary condition for watermarking.

Prior work found that distances between queries made during model extraction attacks follow a different distribution than the legitimate ones [9]. Thus, attacks could be detected using density estimation methods, where $\mathcal{A}$'s inputs produce a highly skewed distribution. This technique protects DNN models against specific attacks using synthetic queries and does not generalize to other attacks, e.g. Knockoff nets. Other methods are designed to detect queries that explore abnormally large region of the input space [11] or attempt to identify queries that get increasingly close to the classes' decision boundaries [25]. However, these techniques are limited in application to decision trees and they are ineffective against complex DNNs that are targeted by Knockoff nets.

In this work, we aim to detect queries that significantly deviate from the distribution of victim's dataset without affecting prediction API's performance. As such, our approach is closest to the PRADA [9] defense. However, we aim to detect Knockoff nets, which PRADA is not designed for. Our defense exploits the fact that Knockoff nets uses natural images sampled from public databases constructed for a general task. Our defense presents an inexpensive, yet effective defense against Knockoff nets, and may have wide practical applicability. However, we believe that ML-based detection schemes open up the possibility of evasion, which we aim to investigate in future work.

7   Conclusion

We evaluated the effectiveness of Knockoff nets, a state-of-the-art model extraction attack, in several real-life scenarios. We showed that under its original adversary model described in [22], it is possible to detect an adversary $\mathcal{A}$ mounting Knockoff nets attacks by distinguishing between in- and out-of-distribution queries. While we confirm the results reported in [22], we also showed that more realistic assumptions about the capabilities of $\mathcal{A}$ can have both positive and negative implications for attack effectiveness. On the one hand, the performance of Knockoff nets is reduced against more realistic prediction APIs that do not return complete probability vector. On the other hand, if $\mathcal{A}$ knows the task of the victim model and has access to sufficient unlabeled data drawn from the same distribution as the $\mathcal{V}$'s training data, it can not only be very effective, but virtually undetectable. We therefore conclude that strong, but realistic adversary can extract complex real-life DNN models effectively, without being detected. Given this conclusion, we believe that deterrence techniques like watermarking [28] and fingerprinting [21] deserve further study – while they cannot prevent model extraction, they can reduce the incentive for model extraction by rendering large-scale exploitation of extracted models detectable.

Acknowledgments. This work was supported in part by Intel (ICRI-CARS). We would like to thank Aalto Science-IT project for computational resources.

References

1. Biggio, B., et al.: One-and-a-half-class multiple classifier systems for secure learning against evasion attacks at test time. In: Schwenker, F., Roli, F., Kittler, J. (eds.) MCS 2015. LNCS, vol. 9132, pp. 168–180. Springer, Cham (2015). https://doi.org/10.1007/978-3-319-20248-8_15
2. Bishop, C.M.: Pattern Recognition and Machine Learning. Information Science and Statistics. Springer, Heidelberg (2006)

3. Correia-Silva, J.R., Berriel, R.F., Badue, C., de Souza, A.F., Oliveira-Santos, T.: Copycat CNN: stealing knowledge by persuading confession with random non-labeled data. In: International Joint Conference on Neural Networks (IJCNN), pp. 1–8. IEEE (2018)
4. Deng, J., Dong, W., Socher, R., Jia Li, L., Li, K., Fei-fei, L.: ImageNet: a large-scale hierarchical image database. In: In CVPR (2009)
5. Griffin, G.S., Holub, A., Perona, P.: Caltech-256 object category dataset (2007)
6. He, K., Zhang, X., Ren, S., Sun, J.: Deep residual learning for image recognition. In: Proceedings of the IEEE Conference on Computer Vision and Pattern Recognition, pp. 770–778 (2016)
7. Hendrycks, D., Gimpel, K.: A baseline for detecting misclassified and out-of-distribution examples in neural networks. In: Proceedings of International Conference on Learning Representations (2017)
8. Jagielski, M., Carlini, N., Berthelot, D., Kurakin, A., Papernot, N.: High-fidelity extraction of neural network models. arXiv preprint arXiv:1909.01838 (2019)
9. Juuti, M., Szyller, S., Marchal, S., Asokan, N.: PRADA: protecting against DNN model stealing attacks. In: IEEE European Symposium on Security and Privacy (EuroS&P), pp. 1–16. IEEE (2019, to appear)
10. Kaggle: Kaggle diabetic retinopathy detection training dataset (DRD). https://www.kaggle.com/c/diabetic-retinopathy-detection (2015)
11. Kesarwani, M., Mukhoty, B., Arya, V., Mehta, S.: Model extraction warning in MLaaS paradigm. In: Proceedings of the 34th Annual Computer Security Applications Conference. ACM (2018)
12. Kingma, D.P., Ba, J.: Adam: a method for stochastic optimization. arXiv preprint arXiv:1412.6980 (2014)
13. Kornblith, S., Shlens, J., Le, Q.V.: Do better ImageNet models transfer better? arXiv preprint arXiv:1805.08974 (2018)
14. Kornblith, S., Shlens, J., Le, Q.V.: Do better ImageNet models transfer better? In: Proceedings of the IEEE Conference on Computer Vision and Pattern Recognition, pp. 2661–2671 (2019)
15. Krizhevsky, A.: Learning multiple layers of features from tiny images (2009)
16. Kuznetsova, A., et al.: The open images dataset v4: unified image classification, object detection, and visual relationship detection at scale. arXiv preprint arXiv:1811.00982 (2018)
17. Lee, K., Lee, K., Lee, H., Shin, J.: A simple unified framework for detecting out-of-distribution samples and adversarial attacks. In: Advances in Neural Information Processing Systems, pp. 7167–7177 (2018)
18. Lee, T., Edwards, B., Molloy, I., Su, D.: Defending against model stealing attacks using deceptive perturbations. arXiv preprint arXiv:1806.00054 (2018)
19. Li, P., Yi, J., Zhang, L.: Query-efficient black-box attack by active learning. arXiv preprint arXiv:1809.04913 (2018)
20. Liang, S., Li, Y., Srikant, R.: Principled detection of out-of-distribution examples in neural networks. arXiv preprint arXiv:1706.02690 (2017)
21. Lukas, N., Zhang, Y., Kerschbaum, F.: Deep neural network fingerprinting by conferrable adversarial examples. arXiv preprint arXiv:1912.00888 (2019)
22. Orekondy, T., Schiele, B., Fritz, M.: Knockoff nets: stealing functionality of black-box models. In: CVPR (2019)
23. Orekondy, T., Schiele, B., Fritz, M.: Prediction poisoning: Utility-constrained defenses against model stealing attacks. In: International Conference on Representation Learning (ICLR) (2020). https://arxiv.org/abs/1906.10908

24. Papernot, N., McDaniel, P., Goodfellow, I., Jha, S., Celik, Z.B., Swami, A.: Practical black-box attacks against machine learning. In: Proceedings of the 2017 ACM on Asia Conference on Computer and Communications Security, pp. 506–519. ACM (2017)

25. Quiring, E., Arp, D., Rieck, K.: Forgotten siblings: unifying attacks on machine learning and digital watermarking. In: IEEE European Symposium on Security and Privacy (EuroS&P), pp. 488–502 (2018)

26. Simonyan, K., Zisserman, A.: Very deep convolutional networks for large-scale image recognition. arXiv preprint arXiv:1409.1556 (2014)

27. Stallkamp, J., Schlipsing, M., Salmen, J., Igel, C.: The German traffic sign recognition benchmark: a multi-class classification competition. In: IEEE International Joint Conference on Neural Networks (2011)

28. Szyller, S., Atli, B.G., Marchal, S., Asokan, N.: Dawn: dynamic adversarial watermarking of neural networks. arXiv preprint arXiv:1906.00830 (2019)

29. TechWorld: How tech giants are investing in artificial intelligence (2019). https://www.techworld.com/picture-gallery/data/tech-giants-investing-in-artificial-intelligence-3629737. Accessed 9 May 2019

30. Torralba, A., Efros, A.A.: Unbiased look at dataset bias. In: CVPR 2011, pp. 1521–1528. IEEE (2011)

31. Tramèr, F., Zhang, F., Juels, A., Reiter, M.K., Ristenpart, T.: Stealing machine learning models via prediction Apis. In: 25th USENIX Security Symposium (USENIX Security 2016), pp. 601–618 (2016)

32. Welinder, P., et al.: Caltech-UCSD Birds 200. Technical report. CNS-TR-2010-001, California Institute of Technology (2010)

33. Yosinski, J., Clune, J., Bengio, Y., Lipson, H.: How transferable are features in deep neural networks? In: Advances in Neural Information Processing Systems, vol. 27, pp. 3320–3328. Curran Associates, Inc. (2014). http://papers.nips.cc/paper/5347-how-transferable-are-features-in-deep-neural-networks.pdf

34. Zhu, C., Byrd, R.H., Lu, P., Nocedal, J.: L-BFGS-B - Fortran subroutines for large-scale bound constrained optimization. Technical report, ACM Transactions on Mathematical Software (1994)

Principal Component Properties
of Adversarial Samples

Malhar Jere[1], Sandro Herbig[2]([⊠]), Christine Lind[1], and Farinaz Koushanfar[1]

[1] University of California San Diego, La Jolla, CA, USA
mjjere@ucsd.edu
[2] University of Erlangen-Nuremberg, Erlagen, Germany
thesandroherbig@gmail.com

Abstract. Deep Neural Networks for image classification have been found to be vulnerable to adversarial samples, which consist of sub-perceptual noise added to a benign image that can easily fool trained neural networks, posing a significant risk to their commercial deployment. In this work, we analyze adversarial samples through the lens of their contributions to the principal components of *each* image, which is different than prior works in which authors performed PCA on the entire dataset. We investigate a number of state-of-the-art deep neural networks trained on ImageNet as well as several attacks for each of the networks. Our results demonstrate empirically that adversarial samples across several attacks have similar properties in their contributions to the principal components of neural network inputs. We propose a new metric for neural networks to measure their robustness to adversarial samples, termed the (k, p) point. We utilize this metric to achieve 93.36% accuracy in detecting adversarial samples independent of architecture and attack type for models trained on ImageNet.

Keywords: Neural networks · Neural network robustness · Adversarial samples

1 Introduction

Artificial Neural Networks have made a resurgence in recent times and have achieved state of the art results on numerous tasks such as image classification [1]. As their popularity rises the investigation of their security will become ever more relevant. Adversarial examples in particular - which involve small, tailored changes to the input to make the neural network misclassify it - pose a serious threat to the safe utilization of neural networks. Recent works have shown that adversarial samples comprise of *non-robust* features of datasets, and that neural networks trained on adversarial samples can generalize to the test set [4]. Because these non-robust features are invisible for humans, performing inference on lossy

Supported by the Semiconductor Research Corporation.

reconstructions of the adversarial input has the potential to shed light on the dependence between the adversarial noise and the robust features of the image.

In this work, we seek to analyze adversarial samples in terms of their contribution to the principal components of an image and characterize the vulnerability of these models. We test our method for a number of different Deep Neural Network architectures, datasets and attack types, and identify a general trend about adversarial samples.

2   Background and Prior Work

2.1   Adversarial Samples

We consider a neural network $f(\cdot)$ used for classification where $f(x)_i$ represents the probability that image x corresponds to class i. Images are represented as $x \in [0,1]^{w.h.c}$, where w, h, c are the width, height and number of channels of the image. We denote the classification of the network as $c(x) = \text{argmax}\, i f(x)_i$, with $c^*(x)$ representing the true class, or the ground truth of the image. Given an image x and an image classifier $f(\cdot)$, an adversarial sample x' follows two properties:

- $D(x, x')$ is small for some distance metric D, implying that the images x and x' appear visually similar to humans.
- $c(x') \neq c^*(x) = c(x)$. This means that the prediction on the adversarial sample is incorrect whereas the original prediction is correct.

In this work, we focus on 3 methods to generate adversarial samples.

DeepFool. Deepfool [8] is an iterative untargeted attack technique to manipulate the decision boundaries of neural networks while minimizing the L_2 distance metric between the altered (adversarial) example and the original image.

Jacobian Saliency Map Attack: Papernot et al. introduced the Jacobian-based Saliency Map Attack [6], a targeted attack optimized under the L_0 distance. The attack is a greedy algorithm that utilizes the *saliency map* of neural networks to pick pixels to modify one at a time, increasing the target classification on each iteration.

Carlini Wagner Attack. For a given image, the goal of the Carlini Wagner attack [7] is to find a small perturbation such that the model misclassifies the input as a chosen adversarial class. The attack can be formulated as the following optimization problem: $min||\delta||_p + c \cdot f(x + \delta)$ such that $x + \delta \in [0,1]^n$ where $||\delta||_p$ is the p-norm. In this paper we use the L_2 norm i.e. $p = 2$.

2.2 Prior Work

There have been several prior works in detecting adversarial samples. DeepFense[2] formalizes the goal of thwarting adversarial attacks as an optimization problem that minimizes the rarely observed regions in the latent feature space spanned by a neural network. [9] seek to minimize the reverse cross-entropy which encourage deep networks to learn latent representations that better distinguish adversarial examples from normal ones. [10] identify exploitation channels and utilize them for adversarial sample detection.

Our work is most similar to [11], which characterizes adversarial samples in terms of the Local Intrinsic Dimensionality, and to [7] and [12], which show PCA to be an effective defense against certain adversarial attacks on smaller datasets such as MNIST. Our method, however, is different in that we seek to understand adversarial samples based on their contributions to the principal components of a *single* image, and that we use the rows as principal components, thereby allowing us to scale our technique to much larger datasets such as ImageNet.

3 Methodology

3.1 Threat Model

There are two different settings for adversarial attacks. The most general setting is the black box threat model where adversaries do not have access to any information about the neural network (e.g. gradient) except for the predictions of the network. In the white box threat model all information about the neural network is accessible, including its weights, architecture, gradients and training method. In this work we consider situations where adversaries have white-box access to the neural network.

3.2 Defensive PCA

[7] and [12] have shown PCA to be an effective defense against certain adversarial attacks on smaller datasets, where n is the number of samples in the dataset and d the number of features (*rows* × *columns*) of each sample. This works well when the dataset and number of features are small, however, for larger datasets with larger inputs this method becomes computationally inefficient as the size of the data matrix scales quadratically with the size of dataset.

To tackle this emerging problem we suggest an alternative way to perform PCA, where $n = w$ is the number of rows and $d = h \times c$ is the product of the number of columns and the channels of an image $x \in [0,1]^{w.h.c}$. In doing so we can capture the correlations between pixels of an image and vastly reduce the number of dimensions required for PCA. Additionally, this method is independent of the dataset size. Furthermore, our method also has the added advantage that it requires no knowledge of the dataset which makes it more versatile.

We term this new method of performing PCA as *rowPCA* denoted as $C = P_{row}(x)$ for an input image $x \in [0,1]^{w.h.c}$, which treats each $h \times c$ row of x as a principal axis. As an example, an ImageNet input image x with dimensionality $(224 \times 224 \times 3)$ will generate 224 principal components. We can then reconstruct our image x from the principal components with smaller components contributing smaller variance to the image. We denote the first i principal components $[c_1, c_2, ...c_i]$ as $C_{1:i}$, and the image reconstruction operation as $P_{inv,row}(\cdot)$. The reconstructed image x^* generated from the first i row principal components is thus $x^* = P_{inv,row}(C_{1:i})$. Figure 1 shows several reconstructed inputs for a benign sample.

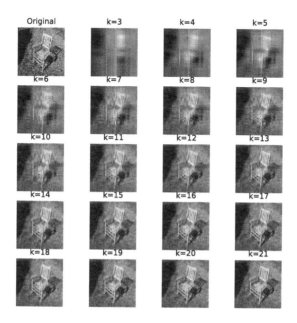

Fig. 1. Examples of PCA reconstructed images for a randomly chosen image from the ImageNet validation dataset.

3.3   Detecting Dominant Classes

We define the dominant class as the predicted class on the full image x. The (k, p) point is defined as a tuple consisting of the component when the dominant class starts becoming the top prediction and the softmax probability p of the dominant class at that particular component number. Algorithm 1 outlines the procedure to obtain the (k, p) point for a particular input, and Fig. 2 demonstrates the functionality of our detection method on an adversarial sample. The steps that occur are:

- The input image is decomposed into its principal components by the rows.
- Each of the sets $C_{1:k}$ of descending principal components (sorted by eigenvalue) is used to reconstruct the image.

- Each reconstructed image is fed through the neural network and the predictions are observed.
- The (k, p) point is found for the particular set of predictions for each image and is subsequently used to determine whether that particular sample is adversarial or benign.

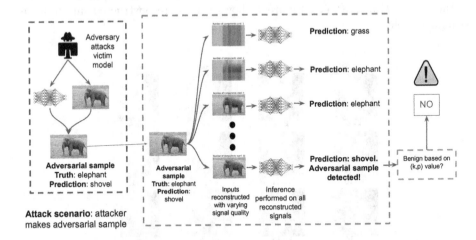

Fig. 2. Visualization of defensive PCA applied to an adversarial input. For an input image, we reconstruct the image from the principal components and perform inference on each to determine the component when the dominant class starts becoming the top prediction. The dominant class could be the adversarial class for adversarial inputs, or the ground truth or misclassified class for benign inputs.

Result: (k, p) point
begin:
$k = n$;
$topper = argmax f(x)$
while $topper == c(x)$ **do**
    $k = k - 1$;
    $x^* = P_{inv,row}(C_{1:k})$
    $topper = argmax f(x^*)$
$p = p(x^*)[topper]$
return(k, p)

Algorithm 1: Finding the (k, p) point for a given neural network $f(\cdot)$, input image x, top scoring class on input image $c(x)$, and maximum number of principal components n. We reconstruct the image from components 1 through i and find the point at which the dominant class is no longer dominant.

4   Experiments

4.1   Experimental Setup

Datasets and Models: We evaluated our method on neural networks pre-trained on the ImageNet dataset [13] in PyTorch, namely Inception-v3, [14], Resnet-50 [15], and VGG19 [16].

Attack Methods: For each of the models we evaluated our method on the DeepFool [8], Jacobian Saliency Map Attack (JSMA) [6] and Carlini-Wagner L2 attack [7] using the Foolbox library [3]. For each of the 9 *(attack, model)* pairs, we generated 100 adversarial images.

4.2   Results

Behavior of Adversarial Samples. Figures 3a, 3b and 3c shows the clustering of adversarial samples in similar regions of the (k, p) space, while Fig. 3d shows the clustering of benign samples in similar regions of the (k, p) space. Figure 4 shows the (k, p) points of all the adversarial and benign points, demonstrating their separability.

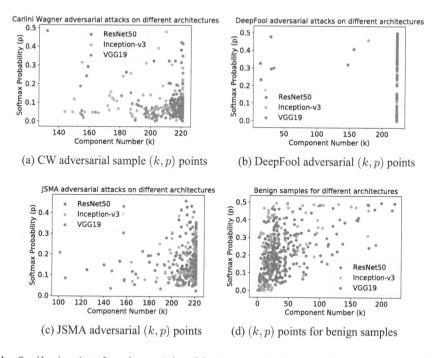

(a) CW adversarial sample (k, p) points   (b) DeepFool adversarial (k, p) points

(c) JSMA adversarial (k, p) points   (d) (k, p) points for benign samples

Fig. 3. (k, p) points for adversarial and benign samples for ImageNet trained models.

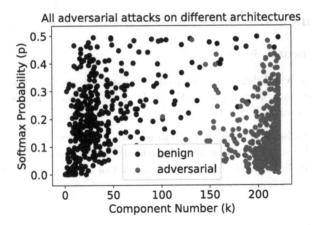

Fig. 4. (k, p) points for all benign and adversarial ImageNet samples for all models and adversarial attacks.

Detection of Adversarial Samples. We train binary classifiers on the (k, p) points for a fixed *(attack, model)* pair and evaluate them against points from the same pair as well as adversarial samples derived using other attacks targeted towards different architectures.

- **Intra-model detection rate:** Given a *(attack, model)* pair, this metric measures the probability of predicting whether a given (k, p) point is either a benign or adversarial sample. We gathered 128 correctly-predicted benign samples and 100 adversarial points for each *(attack, model)* pair for the ImageNet dataset and used an AdaBoost [17] classifier with 200 weak Decision Tree estimators to distinguish between the two. We achieve an average prediction rate of 94.81%, namely that we can correctly predict whether a sample for a given neural network will be adversarial or benign 94.81% of the time.
- **Inter-model detection rate:** We observe the (k, p) distributions of adversarial samples across all attack types and models in order to determine their similarity. To measure this, we train classifiers trained on one *(attack, model)* pair and evaluate them on benign and adversarial samples for every other *(attack, model)* pair, as demonstrated in Fig. 5. We achieve an average adversarial detection rate of 93.36% across all architectures and adversarial methods.

5   Discussion

PCA is one of numerous linear methods for dimensionality reduction of neural network inputs. Other techniques such as Sparse Dictionary Learning and Local Linear Embedding are potential alternatives to PCA, which we intend on exploring in future work. One particular limitation of our method is the need for many rows in the input, which would make our defense inapplicable to inputs for smaller neural networks.

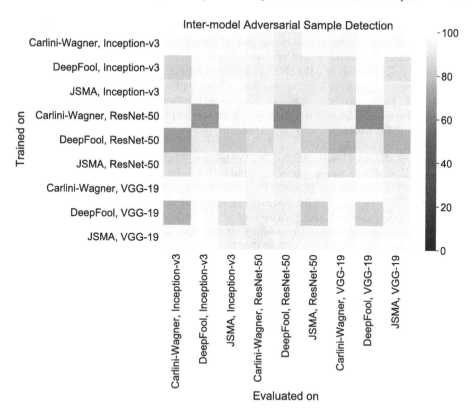

Fig. 5. Inter-model and Intra-model adversarial sample detection. We achieve near perfect prediction rates for simple discriminative models trained to identify adversarial samples from one *(attack, model)* pair and evaluated on a different one. The y axis represents the *(attack, model)* we trained our classifier to identify, and the x axis represents the *(attack, model)* we evaluated our classifier on.

6   Conclusion

We identify a new metric, the (k, p) point, to analyze adversarial samples in terms of their contributions to the principal components of an image. We demonstrate empirically that the (k, p) points of benign and adversarial samples are distinguishable across adversarial attacks and neural network architectures and are an underlying property of the dataset itself. We train a binary classifier to detect adversarial samples and achieve a 93.36% detection success rate.

References

1. Russakovsky, O., et al.: ImageNet large scale visual recognition challenge. Int. J. Comput. Vis. **115**(3), 211–252 (2015)

2. Rouhani, B.D., Samragh, M., Javaheripi, M., Javidi, T., Koushanfar, F.: Deep-Fense: online accelerated defense against adversarial deep learning. In: IEEE/ACM International Conference on Computer-Aided Design (ICCAD), pp. 1–8

3. Rauber, J., Brendel, W., Bethge, M.: Foolbox: a python toolbox to benchmark the robustness of machine learning models. arXiv preprint 1707.04131 (2017)

4. Ilyas, A., Santurkar, S., Tsipras, D., Engstrom, L., Tran, B., Madry, A.: Adversarial examples are not bugs, they are features. arXiv preprint arXiv:1905.02175 (2019)

5. Brown, T.B., Mané, D., Roy, A., Abadi, M., Gilmer, J.: Adversarial patch. arXiv preprint :1712.09665 (2017)

6. Papernot, N., McDaniel, P., Jha, S., Fredrikson, M., Celik, Z.B., Swami, A.: The limitations of deep learning in adversarial settings. In: IEEE European Symposium on Security and Privacy (EuroS&P), pp. 372–387 (2016)

7. Carlini, N., Wagner, D.: Adversarial examples are not easily detected: bypassing ten detection methods. In: Proceedings of the 10th ACM Workshop on Artificial Intelligence and Security. Proceedings of the 10th ACM Workshop on Artificial Intelligence and Security, pp. 3–14 (2017)

8. Moosavi-Dezfooli, S.-M., Fawzi, A., Frossard, P.: DeepFool: a simple and accurate method to fool deep neural networks. In: Proceedings of the IEEE Conference on Computer Vision and Pattern Recognition, pp. 2574–2582 (2016)

9. Pang, T., Du, C., Dong, Y., Zhu, J.: Towards robust detection of adversarial examples. In: Advances in Neural Information Processing Systems, pp. 4579–4589 (2018)

10. Ma, S., Liu, Y., Tao, G.. Lee, W.-C., Zhang, X.: NIC: detecting adversarial samples with neural network invariant checking. In: Proceedings of the 26th Network and Distributed System Security Symposium (NDSS) (2019)

11. Ma, X., et al.: Characterizing adversarial subspaces using local intrinsic dimensionality. arXiv preprint 1801.02613 (2018)

12. Bhagoji, A.N., Cullina, D., Mittal, P.: Dimensionality reduction as a defense against evasion attacks on machine learning classifiers (2017)

13. Deng, J., Dong, W., Socher, R., Li, L.-J., Li, K., Fei-Fei, L.: ImageNet: a large-scale hierarchical image database. In: 2009 IEEE Conference on Computer Vision and Pattern Recognition, pp. 248–255 (2009)

14. Szegedy, C., Vanhoucke, V., Ioffe, S., Shlens, J., Wojna, Z.: Rethinking the inception architecture for computer vision. In: Proceedings of the IEEE Conference on Computer Vision and Pattern Recognition, pp. 2818–2826 (2016)

15. He, K., Zhang, X., Ren, S., Sun, J.: Deep residual learning for image recognition. In: Proceedings of the IEEE Conference on Computer Vision and Pattern Recognition, pp. 770–778 (2016)

16. Simonyan, K., Zisserman, A.: Very deep convolutional networks for large-scale image recognition. arXiv preprint:1409.1556 (2014)

17. Freund, Y., Schapire, R.: A short introduction to boosting. J. Jpn. Soc. Artif. Intell. **14**, 771–780 (1999)

FreaAI: Automated Extraction of Data Slices to Test Machine Learning Models

Samuel Ackerman, Orna Raz$^{(\boxtimes)}$, and Marcel Zalmanovici

IBM Research, Haifa, Israel
ornar@il.ibm.com

Abstract. Although machine learning (ML) solutions are prevalent, in order for them to be truly 'business-grade' and reliable, their performance must be shown to be robust for many different data subsets observations with similar feature values (which we call 'slices') which they are expected to encounter in deployment. However, ML solutions are often evaluated only based on aggregate performance (e.g., overall accuracy) and not on the variability on various slices. For example, a text classifier deployed on bank terms may have very high accuracy (e.g., $98\% \pm 2\%$) but might perform poorly for the data slice of terms that include short descriptions and originate from commercial accounts. Yet a business requirement may be for the classifier to perform well regardless of the text characteristics. In previous work [1] we demonstrated the effectiveness of using feature-based analysis to highlight such gaps in performance assessment. Here we demonstrate a novel technique, called IBM FreaAI, which automatically extracts explainable feature slices for which the ML solution's performance is statistically significantly worse than the average. We demonstrate results of evaluating ML classifier models on seven open datasets.

1 Introduction

Software systems that utilize ML are becoming more and more prevalent. The quality of ML-based solutions greatly depends on the data used to train a solution. Common approaches for assessing the quality of trained ML solutions (we will refer to these as ML) use the average performance of the ML according to some metric, such as accuracy or F1-score for a classifier and R^2 or root mean square error (RMSE) for regression, over unseen yet representative data, such as that of a test set. Of course, even if these average measures are satisfactory, there are likely to exist data records for which the ML performance is far below the average. It is important to understand this behavior as these far-away records might be indicative of unmet requirements. For example, the third row in Table 8 indicates that the ML model trained over loan approval data (the **Adult** dataset) under-performs for people in the ages of 33 to 64. While the overall accuracy is roughly 85%, the accuracy for people in this age group is roughly 80%. Probably this fails to meet a requirement of providing similar ML performance regardless of age. Another example in that table is under-performance of roughly 67% accuracy for people who work 40 to 43 h per week and belong to workclass category

© Springer Nature Switzerland AG 2020
O. Shehory et al. (Eds.): EDSMLS 2020, CCIS 1272, pp. 67–83, 2020.
https://doi.org/10.1007/978-3-030-62144-5_6

5. It is probably required that the solution be insensitive to the number of hours a person works and their workclass. These are examples of 'data slices'. The first is a single feature data slice and the second is a 2-way feature interaction data slice.

In previous work [1] we showed that data slices, defined by a Combinatorial Testing (CT) feature model, result in identifying far-away records in a way that a user can understand and act upon. In that work the feature models were defined manually, and included various abstractions of the ML input data as well as additional metadata. In this work we concentrate on automatically creating feature models for one simple yet useful type of abstraction—that of binning input data feature values. The next section provides background about feature models.

While searching over single categorical feature values to find interesting slices is straightforward, searching over continuous-valued features and over interactions of multiple features is challenging. An exhaustive search is infeasible as the search space is exponential. Moreover, reporting such records or data slices should be done such that the user can take corrective actions. This means that the user needs to understand what defines a data slice. FreaAI is our novel technology that implements a set of heuristics to efficiently suggest data slices that are, by construction, explainable, correct, and statistically significant. 'Explainable' means that data slices are described solely as ranges or single values and their unions. FreaAI is named after the Norse goddess Frea (spelling varies) who, among other traits, can foresee the future, but does not share this knowledge with humans. Our technology suggests data slices that are correct, yet the results may be incomplete in that not all possible under-performing slices may be found.

The contribution of this paper is a set of heuristics for automatically defining feature models, such that each slice in that model is indicative of ML under-performance, is statistically significant, and can be easily understood by a human. We validate these heuristics by analyzing seven open datasets. FreaAI generates data slices that contain significantly more mis-predicted data records than would be expected by randomly drawing the same number of data records.

We next list related work and provide background from our previous work about feature models and data slices. The methodology of heuristically and automatically suggesting data slices and the definition of our requirements from data slices are then presented. The experimental results of running our technology on seven open data-sets follow, and we conclude with a discussion and brief summary of the contributions of this work.

2   Related Work and Background

Several works capture challenges and best practices in developing ML solutions, e.g., [2,10,13], or suggest organizational work-flows for building successful AI projects [9].

We summarize the most relevant background and results from our previous work [1]. The work we report on in here is motivated by that work. In a nutshell, we suggested the use of CT modeling methodology for validating ML solutions. Building on that work, here we report on FreaAI, a novel technology for automatically extracting feature models, which are an instance of CT models, out of ML data, implementing an abstraction of automated binning according to ML performance.

Following are more details on our previous work. We demonstrated that the Combinatorial modeling methodology is a viable approach for gaining actionable insights on the quality of ML solutions. Applying the approach results in identifying coverage gaps indicating uncovered requirements. The approach also identifies under-performing slices, suggesting areas where the current ML model cannot be relied upon. When used in the development stage of the ML solution life-cycle, the approach can also suggest additional training data or the inclusion of multiple ML model variants as part of the overall ML solution. The methodology may also assist in directing the labeling effort to areas that would best cover the business requirements. That work utilized the modeling process used by CT [3–6,8,11,12] to detect weak business areas of the ML solution and strengthen them.

CT is a well-known testing technique to achieve a small and effective test plan. The systematic combinatorial modeling methodology used by CT provides insight on the business requirements and ties them to testing artifacts. We utilized the combinatorial model as a means to detect gaps and weaknesses of the ML solution. Business requirements often do not appear as features in the ML solution training data. Rather, they can be defined as abstractions over these features or may utilize additional information that is not always available for learning. The CT model parameters may then include abstractions as simple as dividing values into bins, such as defining ranges over age as young, middle-aged and elderly, as well as more complex abstractions such as defining mathematical functions over the relation between multiple features.

Using the mapping between CT model parameters and ML model features, we defined *data slices* over the training data as follows. We observed that a t-way interaction coverage requirement induces a division of the training data into slices. Each slice corresponds to a specific value combination of size t and consists of all data records that map to that specific value combination. Naturally, the number of data slices is equal to the number of t-way value combinations in the CT model. Note that the slices are not disjoint, since each data record maps to multiple value combinations of size t, reflecting different business requirements that it captures. Data slices over credit data may include records that belong to young women (a 1-way interaction slice) and records that belong to young women with only high-school level education (a 2-way interaction slice). We performed coverage gap analysis of the training data associated with each data slice. Slices with no corresponding training data expose business areas in which the ML solution will likely under-perform. For slices with sufficient data or support, we computed the ML metric over each slice. We expected the result for a slice to be within the confidence interval of the ML metric over the entire data. If that was not the case, we highlighted the slice as indicative of business requirements that are not well addressed by the ML solution.

The work we report on here provides a set of heuristics, FreaAI, for applying the above CT modeling methodology on the ML solution test data in order to better validate it and verify that it addresses its requirements. As even the simple abstractions were shown to be useful, FreaAI was designed to automatically generate simple abstractions such as binning of continuous features and identification of categorical feature values and combinations of feature. The resulting data slices are guaranteed to: (1) under-perform relative to the overall ML solution performance, (2) be explainable, (3) be statistically significant. Details on the heuristics and how they guarantee these properties follow in the Methodology Section.

3   Methodology

FreaAI automatically analyzes features and feature interactions in order to define feature models in which each of the data slices under-performs. It requires only the test data and the ML prediction for each record, without requiring knowledge of the ML model, for instance.

3.1   Single Feature Analysis

FreaAI starts by analyzing single features. The rationale is that the simpler the reason for an issue, the easier it is to understand its cause and, as a result, easier to come up with a fix. FreaAI heuristically decides which features should be treated as categorical and which as continuous and does so automatically based on the type of feature data and number of unique values. Alternatively, the user can supply this information. Looking for under-performing data slices over single categorical features is simple. FreaAI computes the ML performance of data slices that are defined by each of the feature possible values (categories). Finding data slices over single continuous features is challenging, as we need a way to find interesting ranges. We do that in various ways, explained in the following paragraphs.

3.2   Feature Interactions Analysis

FreaAI also analyzes feature interactions. It does so in two ways: (1) by slicing on a category or range found when analyzing a single feature and repeating the process for a single feature on that subset, or (2) by using a method which can divide the search space on multiple axis at once—in our case, a decision tree (DT) on n features. From CT we know that most software problems involve a small number of variables. Empirically, we notice that this seems to be the case for data features used for ML as well; single features and interactions of two or three features already uncover many problems. An inherent problem with increasing the interaction level is that the higher the interaction level, the less likely it is to have sufficient support.

3.3 Heuristics for Feature and Interaction Analysis

We experimented with multiple feature-analysis techniques. These included clustering methods, building decision trees, and Highest Posterior Density (HPD), also known as High Density Regions (HDR) [7] to extract feature models with under-performing slices. We shortly describe each of the techniques. We found decision trees and HPD to be the most effective, therefore we report only on the results of applying these heuristics in the Experimental Results section.

Clustering as a Feature Analysis Heuristic. We applied clustering techniques to group the test data. We utilized multiple clustering algorithms that are inherently different in concept, such as k-means and DBScan. We then tested whether any of the resulting clusters exhibited ML under-performance. We also varied the clustering metric and the parameters to get different clusters. While this method worked well for identifying under-performing slices, it was hard to automatically point out the offending feature(s) in a way that was user-actionable. We could only mark a (small) subset of features as being more dominant in the under-performing cluster than in the rest of the test set, suggesting one or more of them could be responsible.

HPD as a Feature Analysis Heuristic. HPD is a nonparametric method that computes the shortest possible interval or union of non-overlapping intervals containing a given proportion of records in a univariate and numeric sample; it

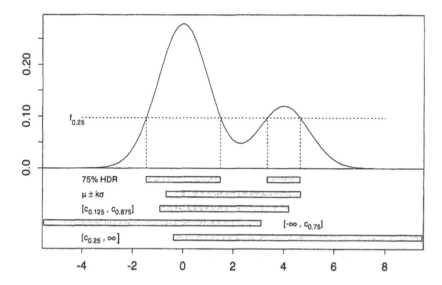

Fig. 1. Illustration of five different intervals containing 75% of the density from an example (bimodal) empirical sample (source: [7]). The first one is the HDR (or HPD) since of the five, it is the shortest (highest-density); in this case, the HPD is given by a union of two non-overlapping intervals due to the bimodality of the distribution.

essentially gives the 'best possible' empirical confidence interval for a sample. An illustration from the original paper is given in Fig. 1.

Since HPDs can only be used on univariate numeric data (unlike decision trees, which do not have such restrictions), we use it in our heuristic only to identify interesting slices for each numeric feature alone (i.e., no higher-order interactions). So the slices are explainable and to avoid potential overfitting due to multi-modality of the distribution, we furthermore restrict the HPD to consist of a single interval, rather than a union. For the sample of each relevant feature in the test dataset, we begin by finding the initial HPD, and iteratively shrink that area by some epsilon (typically 0.05) checking whether the performance on the new sample increases or decreases relative to the previous one. If it decreases, then we have found a smaller range which under-performs. Alternatively, if it increases, then at least one of the discarded ranges (one on either side) under-performs. This process is repeated after dropping the highest-density range from the feature until we remain with too little data, e.g. 10% of the data records.

Figure 2 depicts one iteration of the HPD heuristic over one feature, '*MFCCs_22*' from the **Anuran (family)** dataset. First, the area under the probability density curve, up to and including the vertical ranges, is identified by HPD as containing 90% of the probability density. Our HPD heuristic iteration shrinks that area by 5% by removing the vertical ranges and re-checks the performance of the updated range. It then proceeds as described above.

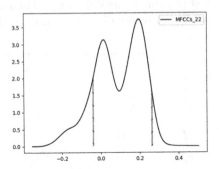

Fig. 2. Shows the areas discarded when changing HPD to include 85% [−0.04553 to 0.26878 with a performance of 0.9858] instead of 90% [−0.07738 to 0.27257 with 0.9840] density. The two marked bars are the areas FreaAI checks when the performance of the lower density is higher. This data belongs to feature '*MFCCs_22*' from **Anuran (family)**.

Decision Trees as a Feature Analysis Heuristic. The decision trees heuristic works as follows. For each subset of one, two or three features the heuristic defines a decision tree classification problem using these features as input. The output is always defined by a binary target of True/False. 'True' means that the original ML model predicted the original output successfully and 'False' means that it failed in its prediction. Notice that this makes each classification problem binary, regardless of the number of original labels. The decision tree heuristic then fits a decision tree model to each of the above training data, but ignores the performance of the resulting model. Instead, it walks the generated tree looking for splits where the purity of 'False' is high enough for the slice defined by it to be under-performing and keeps only those.

Minimal Support. The slicing heuristics consider as candidates only slices that have at least minimum support. Minimum support is heuristically calculated as the maximum between 2 and 0.5% of mis-predicted instances in the test dataset. The rationale is that in a dataset with a high metric performance there will be few mis-predictions, therefore a slice with a small number of mis-predictions is important, whereas for a model whose performance is relatively low there will be many mis-predictions requiring a slice to have more mis-predictions to be interesting. In addition, by taking a percentage we automatically adjust to different test dataset sizes, e.g., Table 1 shows that the **Statlog** dataset has 300 records, while the **Adult** dataset has over 14,000 records. The percentage is user-configurable. However, in our experiments the empirical values that we chose were satisfactory.

3.4   Defining Data Slices Requirements

We define the following requirements from the data slices reported by FreaAI, regardless of the heuristic that generated a data slice. A data slice must be

1. correct,
2. statistically significant, and
3. explainable.

We use a methodology that abides to these requirements and generates slices which are correct-by-construction. The slices are correct because they are subsets of the test set for which we run the same performance metric as on the original dataset. They are statistically significant because we take only slices where the performance is considerably (4% by default) lower than the expected lower-bound of the confidence interval of the performance metric. FreaAI further reports only on data slices that have both minimal support and a sufficiently low p-value, as computed by the hypergeometric distribution test, described in the Experimental Results section. The slices are also self-explainable since they are generated from an easily defined range on a small number of features. Moreover, since we focus on structured datasets with engineered features, the ML model developer should be able to draw useful conclusions. Table 8 lists a few examples of data slices. These are explainable by the way they are defined. For example, the first data slice indicates a problem in the Adult ML model performance when the 'relationship' category is 10. This is an example of a 1-way or single feature data slice. Another data slice indicates a problem when the feature 'hours_per_week' has values between 40 and 43 and the feature 'workclass' category is 5. This is an example of a 2-way or feature interactions data slice.

4   Experimental Results

Our experiments demonstrate the ability of our heuristics, as implemented by FreaAI, to find under-performing data slices that are correct, statistically significant, and explainable.

4.1   Input

We tested FreaAI on open-source data sets, six taken from UCI and one from ProPublica. The datasets are **Adult, Avila, Anuran** (Family, Genus, Species targets), **statlog** (German credit data) from UCI and **COMPAS Recidivism Risk Score** from ProPublica.

Table 1 lists some general information about the datasets and the performance of the models trained on them. We made no attempt at creating the best possible model for each dataset as it is not the goal of this work. We trained a random forest model for each dataset and got ML performance that was similar to the reported performance of each in the literature.

Table 1. Information about the datasets that we tested, listing the number of **test** records, the model performance measured by accuracy and the low/high bounds of the confidence interval for the accuracy

Dataset	# records	Acc	Low CI	High CI
Adult	14653	0.852	0.845	0.857
Avila	6169	0.979	0.976	0.983
Anuran (family)	2159	0.980	0.974	0.987
Anuran (genus)	2159	0.967	0.959	0.974
Anuran (species)	2159	0.969	0.962	0.977
Statlog	300	0.763	0.708	0.821
ProPublica	1852	0.742	0.718	0.759

In our experiments, FreaAI gets as input a test dataset. This is data that was not used for training the ML model, is considered representative of the underlying data distribution, and contains both the ground truth value of the target feature as well as the ML model output, either a numeric or class prediction as appropriate.

4.2   Finding Under-Performing Data Slices

FreaAI implements various slicing heuristics to find candidate under-performing data slices, as discussed in the Methodology Section. FreaAI computes the performance by comparing the ground truth and the ML model prediction that are provided as part of the input data, according to the same ML performance metric used to assess the ML model performance. For simplicity, in all the experiments that we report on here we use accuracy as the ML performance metric and treat all features as numeric. As the Methodology Section explains, we report on the data slices resulting from applying the HPD and the DT slicing heuristics.

FreaAI's heuristics consider as candidates only slices that have at least minimum support, as the Methodology section describes. The candidate slices are further filtered according to their statistical significance and FreaAI reports only on statistically significant slices. The next subsection provides details about the hypergeometric distribution test that FreaAI applies to achieve that.

Tables 4, 5, 6 and 7 show that regardless of the heuristic used to calculate the slices (HPD or DT) or the level of feature interaction (1-way or 2-way), the support varies greatly for all datasets, with the occasional exception of the **Statlog** dataset which is the smallest dataset (see dataset statistics in Table 1). This is to be expected, as our goal is to find groups of mis-predicted records for which we can automatically provide a readable explanation. Table 8 provides examples from the Adult dataset of under-performing data slices.

It is highly encouraging that our heuristics consistently find under-performing data slices. Moreover, the reported slices often have substantial support, increasing the usefulness of the report to the user (Tables 2 and 3).

Table 2. Summary of the number of under-performing slices for 1 and 2-way feature interaction and their total. 'cand' indicates the candidates found the **HPD** heuristic. 'rep' indicates how many candidate slices were actually reported out of the 'cand' list after applying the hypergeometric distribution test with p-value < 0.05.

Dataset	# 1-way		# 2-way		# total	
	cand	rep	cand	rep	cand	rep
Adult	26	25	82	82	**108**	**107**
Avila	38	29	17	17	**55**	**46**
Anuran (family)	80	58	386	371	**466**	**429**
Anuran (genus)	105	61	723	638	**828**	**699**
Anuran (species)	91	64	653	569	**744**	**633**
Statlog	24	7	56	25	**80**	**32**
ProPublica	12	4	13	7	**25**	**11**

Table 3. Summary of the number of under-performing slices for 1 and 2-way feature interaction and their total. 'cand' indicates the candidates found the **DT** (decision trees) heuristic. 'rep' indicates how many candidate slices were actually reported out of the 'cand' list after applying the hypergeometric distribution test with p-value < 0.05.

Dataset	# 1-way		# 2-way		# total	
	cand	rep	cand	rep	cand	rep
Adult	36	35	285	271	**321**	**306**
Avila	120	84	928	689	**1048**	**773**
Anuran (family)	148	113	1539	1265	**1687**	**1378**
Anuran (genus)	209	142	2123	1498	**2332**	**1640**
Anuran (species)	205	134	1881	1336	**2086**	**1470**
Statlog	29	8	610	177	**639**	**185**
ProPublica	1	1	24	22	**25**	**23**

Table 4. Summary of the support for 1-way HPD slices using a stricter p-value in the hypergeometric distribution test of 0.01 as threshold. The first column lists the number of reported slices. Then for each dataset the minimal ('MIN'), average ('AVG'), maximal ('MAX') and standard deviation ('STD') for the reported slices.

Dataset	#	MIN	AVG	MAX	STD
Adult	19	108	2601.5	9888	2931
Avila	13	6	121.1	305	77.6
Anuran (family)	32	2	109.3	197	51.9
Anuran (genus)	36	3	161.1	351	70.2
Anuran (species)	30	3	201.6	460	111.3
Statlog	2	3	78.5	80	1.5
ProPublica	3	24	485.7	942	341.9

Table 5. Summary of the support for 2-way HPD slices using a stricter p-value of 0.01 as a threshold.

Dataset	#	MIN	AVG	MAX	STD
Adult	81	108	1278.7	8749	1741.6
Avila	10	6	28.2	137	37
Anuran (family)	280	2	12.92	92	13.8
Anuran (genus)	351	3	23	114	22.7
Anuran (species)	391	3	31.1	231	37.5
Statlog	11	3	11.82	29	7.1
ProPublica	3	24	143	285	102.8

4.3   Slice Significance Testing

Our combinatorial procedure, along with the HPD and DT heuristics, return data slices of combinations of 1–3 features, that is subsets of the test set records, for which the model performance is worse than the performance on the test set overall. The performance on these slices may not be significantly worse, however. That is, in the case of a classifier, the proportion of correctly-classified observations in these subsets may not be statistically significantly lower than the proportion in the test set overall. Due to the number of potential combinations, which grows polynomially with the number of features, we wish to only return to the user slices with statistically-significantly worse performance than the ML model overall performance.

To assess this, let the test dataset consist of N records, of which $K \in \{0, \ldots, N\}$ are correctly classified. Consider a slice of $n \in \{1, \ldots, N\}$ records, of which $k \in \{0, \ldots, n\}$ are correctly classified. The model under-performance (accuracy k/n) on the slice is considered significant if k is low relative to $n\frac{K}{N}$, the expected number of correctly-classified observation in a randomly drawn subset the same size n from the test set, which has overall accuracy K/N.

Table 6. Summary of the support for 1-way DT slices using a stricter p-value of 0.01 as a threshold.

Dataset	#	MIN	AVG	MAX	STD
Adult	22	108	2301.5	9941	2869
Avila	44	6	55.8	236	51.4
Anuran (family)	70	2	54.6	262	57.9
Anuran (genus)	72	3	74	348	78.4
Anuran (species)	71	3	73.4	451	100.1
Statlog	4	3	80	124	30.1
ProPublica	1	24	519	519	0

Table 7. Summary of the support for 2-way DT slices using a stricter p-value of 0.01 as a threshold.

Dataset	#	MIN	AVG	MAX	STD
Adult	202	108	2682.5	10736	3086.8
Avila	368	6	75.4	366	66.9
Anuran (family)	870	2	71	366	70.3
Anuran (genus)	934	3	92.3	555	90.3
Anuran (species)	818	3	104.1	582	111
Statlog	86	3	87	176	41.2
ProPublica	17	24	372.9	826	220.4

The Hypergeometric Distribution Test. We use the discrete statistical hypergeometric distribution, which in a general setup models the probability of a certain number of binary outcomes (k) from a random draw without replacement of a certain size (n) from a finite population (of size N). In our work, we are concerned with how many correct classifications (a binary outcome) are expected in a random observation subset of a given size (n) from the test set (size N) with a total number K of correct classifications. This likelihood is the probability mass function of the hypergeometric distribution with parameters N, n, K which are observed in the slice, that is, $\Pr(X = x \mid N, n, K)$. The lower-tailed p-value, which evaluates the significance of our result, is simply $\sum_{x=0}^{k} \Pr(X = x \mid N, n, K)$, below the observed correct classification count k in the slice.

Figure 3 illustrates the hypergeometric calculation for the **statlog** on the slice of observations with feature value '*credithistory*'= 5 (not shown in this paper). The slice contains $n = 21$ observations, of which $k = 14$ (66.7%) are correctly classified; the dataset overall has $N = 300$ observations, of which $K = 230$ (76.7%) are correct. The hypergeometric distribution, which models the probability of x correct classifications out of n, in this case has support on $x = \{0, \dots, 21\}$. The dashed line (at 16.1, or 76.7% of 21) indicates the number of correct classifications that would be expected for a random draw of size $n = 21$, that is, the k giving same accuracy as on the test set overall.

Table 8. Examples of under-performing slices taken from both the HPD and the DT heuristics on the **Adult** dataset. The average performance for **Adult** is roughly 0.85. The first 4 rows are examples of 1-way under-performing slices and the last 3 of 2-way slices. The first two rows represent categorical features, the next two continuous features, as decided by heuristic, and the following three come from the union of continuous feature ranges. Note that the last row represents a subset of the range in the third row, i.e. a slice on a secondary feature.

ATTR	VALUE	SUP	PERF	p-val
relationship	5	692	0.699	1.2E−25
education	10	174	0.707	7.4E−07
age	33–64	8538	0.797	1E−113
capital_gain	3942–4934	122	0.688	3.8E−06
(hours_per_week, workclass)	40–43, 5	141	0.673	8.2E−08
(education_num, relationship)	(15, 16), (1, 2, 3, 4)	122	0.680	1.4E−06
(age, hours_per_week)	33–64, 41–99	3019	0.749	1.3E−62

Since we are only dealing with cases where the performance is less than expected (k observed $< n\frac{K}{N}$), the p-value (shown in red in Fig. 3) is the area to the left of the observed value $k = 14$. The performance is not below the expected value significantly enough, however, as the p-value ≈ 0.193. In order to achieve a significant p-value (below 0.05), we would need $k \leq 12$ (accuracy at most 57.1%), indicated by the dotted line. As discussed below, among slices with the same accuracy k/n, the hypergeometric p-value gives more significance to larger slices (n larger). Thus, a slice where $k = 28$ and $n = 42$—both doubled from before, thus leaving the slice accuracy, and the overall K and N unchanged—would have a p-value of ≈ 0.04 and *would* be significant. To have the same significance, in terms of the p-value, as the actual slice, this larger slice would have about 29 correct classifications (69%), that is, *more than twice* the observed $k = 14$. This means that our original slice of size $n = 21$ and accuracy 66.7% is about as significantly as bad as a slice twice as large but with a slightly better accuracy of 69%.

Potential Issues in Computing Significant Slices. Our slicing heuristics require the slices to consist of *all* the records with the set of given categorical feature values, or of all records with numeric feature values in a given range, or

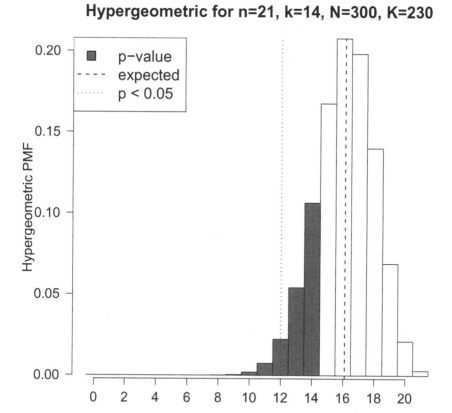

Fig. 3. Hypergeometric distribution of correct classifications and p-value (≈ 0.193) for a slice of size $n = 21$ based on the '*credithistory*' feature of the **statlog** dataset.

to be a higher-order interaction of such single-feature slices. By virtue of this restriction, not all possible random subsets of size n of records would qualify as a slice, if there were omitted observations that would occupy the same range along one of the features. The ML performance on an unconstrained random sample would be on average the same as that on the test set overall. It is possible that, this constraint on the relevant subsets inherently results in ML model performances on the slice that are typically more different from the overall performance than the typical random subset is. This may be investigated in further research. Another issue we will investigate is how to integrate multiple hypothesis testing procedures on the slices. This may need to account for dependence between the model's performance on difference slices due to overlap in the features included, to ensure that slices we identify as significant are so in fact. However, we believe that slices that are filtered out as insignificant using this criterion are definitely not worth investigating further, so this hypergeometric p-value can be considered an initial sanity check on the results.

Selecting Slices with More Support. The procedure of filtering candidate slices based on their low p-values tends to select the larger slices among the candidates as those with worse model performance than the dataset overall. This is a good characteristic of our algorithm, since larger slices tend to indicate more fundamental data issues. Small slices are more likely to represent artefacts of overfitting or simply less-interesting areas of model weakness.

The tendency to select larger slices is a direct result of the hypergeometric distribution, specifically the fact it is based on sampling without replacement from a finite sample (in contrast to the binomial distribution). Given a fixed dataset, the variance of the proportion of correct classifications (that is, of X/n when X is a hypergeometric-distributed random variable) decreases as the sample size (n, here the slice size) increases. Therefore, for two slices with the same performance (i.e., proportion of correct classifications), the larger will be a more significant result; the performance can even be slightly better in the larger slice while still being more significant than the smaller one. For instance, in Table 8 on the **Adult** dataset, the slice based on '$capital\_gain$' has worse model accuracy (0.688) than that based on the 'age' feature (0.797), but has a much smaller slice size ($n = 122$ vs. 8,538). Nevertheless, despite the fact that accuracy on the age slice is better, the larger size makes it a more significant instance of model under-performance, with a much lower p-value, though in this instance both slices have low p-values. A illustrative example of this property is given in the discussion of Fig. 3.

In addition to the variance aspect, which would hold in sampling with replacement, the same level of under-performance is also more significant in a larger slice when sampling without replacement because the slice size is nearer to the finite sample of correctly-classified observations. Thus, the statistical rationale of the p-value reinforces our logical sense that larger diagnostic slices of data are more significant and helpful to the user.

5   Discussion

We report on initial promising results of automatically suggesting under-performing data slices.

In our experiments we applied FreaAI on ML test data. Data slices in general and especially ones automatically generated such as by FreaAI are useful throughout the ML solution development life-cycle. We are working on utilizing data slices from the very early stages of ML solution development, starting from the design of a solution that provides value. We believe that our technology has other useful use cases. One use case may be to identify potential features or feature combinations for de-biasing. Bias is a prejudice that is considered to be unfair, such as refusing a loan based on the gender or race of a person. Even though FreaAI works on existing data which may already be biased and therefore the ML performance on it might be within bounds, FreaAI may occasionally identify data slices that are indicative of bias. Table 9 provides anecdotal evidence of that.

Table 9. Anecdotal relation between FreaAI analysis and features identified as requiring de-biasing. The first two rows are taken from **statlog** in which age <25 was identified as a biasing factor and the next 3 rows from **ProPublica** where number of priors (>1) biases the model. The last two rows show this captured by the DT method which aggregated several values, while the other rows where detected by the HPD method.

ATTR	VALUE	SUP	PERF	p-value
age	21	4	0.250	0.038
age	22	7	0.428	0.045
Number_of_Priors	4	119	0.588	7E−05
Number_of_Priors	5	79	0.658	0.024
Number_of_Priors	3	132	0.659	0.007
age	(19, 20, .., 29)	124	0.670	1E−04
Number_of_Priors	(2, 3, 4, 5)	519	0.660	9E−07

Another use case is to improve the overall ML solution as a result of analyzing the data slices. One may add training data as characterized by data slices or add alternative logic for inputs that belong to specific slices. Computing data slices performance on the training data may assist in doing that. Table 10 provides an example. Slices that have low performance even on the training set and have low support may be indicative of a need for more training data with the slice's characteristics. The first row is an example of that. Slices that have low performance on the training data but high support, such as the second row, may be indicative of a need for alternative logic for input belonging to such slices.

FreaAI can automatically find only issues for which data exists. We highly recommend adding manually-defined validation features to address the challenge of identifying missing requirements.

Table 10. Running FreaAI on the **training** dataset we sometimes encounter slices which under-perform (relative to the train CI) even in this dataset. The higher the model performance the fewer such slices are found. The first two rows in the table are from the **Avila** dataset and the last two from **Anuran (Family)**. The **LOW CI** column is the lower bound of the training dataset confidence interval

ATTR	VALUE	SUP	PERF	p-value	LOW CI
F4	−0.633–0.634	12	0.960	6E−14	0.9992
F3	−2.172–0.18	172	0.988	0	0.9992
MFCCs_4	0.783-1	45	0.977	0	0.9986
MFCCs_9	−0.587–0.311	98	0.989	3E−05	0.9986

There is a challenge of combining and reporting on multiple data slices. We are experimenting with ways to optimize the different factors, such as a Pareto front, to take into account support vs performance, size vs range of a slice and more. We suspect that the use case for which the slices are being analyzed also affects the kind of slices that are more interesting. For example, if our aim is to identify features that should be de-biased, or if it is to direct the labeling effort for getting more training data, we may expect the set of interesting slices suggested by the analysis in these cases to differ from one another.

Using multiple slicing heuristics (e.g., HPD or DT) may result in overlapping slices. This creates a challenge of whether and how to combine the overlapping slices.

We experimented with extracting data slices of up to 3-way feature interactions. It is algorithmically possible to extract slices of any n-way interaction (up to the number of data features). However, we suspect this is not useful because the smaller the dataset is, the more fragmentation the interactions result in and the smaller the likelihood that data exists.

We experimented with multiple heuristics to suggest data slices, and more methods exist. We are exploring ways to rank the resulting slices. Architecturally, to simplify the design, we could use the same method for identifying both 1-way and higher-order interaction slices. This could be done with the DT heuristic, for example. However, it may be the case that different slicing heuristics capture different aspects of unmet requirements. We plan to experiment with prioritizing slices generated with various techniques and develop metrics, including ones based on user feedback, to better estimate the variety of unmet requirements captured.

6   Conclusions

We address the challenge of finding under-performing data slices to validate the ML performance of ML solutions. We developed automated slicing heuristics and implemented them in FreaAI, such that the resulting slices are correct, statistically significant and explainable. We experimented with seven open datasets, demonstrating that FreaAI is able to consistently find under-performing data slices. Moreover, the reported slices often have substantial support, increasing the usefulness of the report to the user.

References

1. Barash, G., Farchi, E., Jayaraman, I., Raz, O., Tzoref-Brill, R., Zalmanovici, M.: Bridging the gap between ML solutions and their business requirements using feature interactions. In: Proceedings of the 2019 27th ACM Joint Meeting on European Software Engineering Conference and Symposium on the Foundations of Software Engineering, pp. 1048–1058. ACM (2019)
2. Breck, E., Cai, S., Nielsen, E., Salib, M., Sculley, D.: What's your ML test score? A rubric for ML production systems. In: Reliable Machine Learning in the Wild - NIPS 2016 Workshop (2016)
3. Burroughs, K., Jain, A., Erickson, R.: Improved quality of protocol testing through techniques of experimental design. In: SUPERCOMM/ICC, pp. 745–752 (1994)
4. Cohen, M.B., Snyder, J., Rothermel, G.: Testing across configurations: implications for combinatorial testing. SIGSOFT Softw. Eng. Notes **31**(6), 1–9 (2006)
5. Dalal, S.R., et al.: Model-based testing in practice. In: ICSE, pp. 285–294 (1999)
6. Grindal, M., Lindström, B., Offutt, J., Andler, S.F.: An evaluation of combination strategies for test case selection. Empirical Softw. Eng. **11**(4), 583–611 (2006)
7. Hyndman, R.J.: Computing and graphing highest density regions. Am. Stat. **50**(2), 120–126 (1996). https://doi.org/10.1080/00031305.1996.10474359. https://www.tandfonline.com/doi/abs/10.1080/00031305.1996.10474359
8. Kuhn, D.R., Kacker, R.N., Lei, Y.: Introduction to Combinatorial Testing. Chapman & Hall/CRC, Boca Raton (2013)
9. Ng, A.: AI transformation playbook how to lead your company into the AI era. Landing AI (2018). https://landing.ai/ai-transformation-playbook/?utm_source=MLYList&utm_medium=TextLink&utm_campaign=Playbook
10. Sculley, D., et al.: Machine learning: the high interest credit card of technical debt. In: SE4ML: Software Engineering for Machine Learning (NIPS 2014 Workshop) (2014)
11. Williams, A.W.: Determination of test configurations for pair-wise interaction coverage. In: TestCom, pp. 59–74 (2000)
12. Wojciak, P., Tzoref-Brill, R.: System level combinatorial testing in practice - the concurrent maintenance case study. In: ICST, pp. 103–112 (2014)
13. Zinkevich, M.: Rules of machine learning: best practices for ML engineering. Google (2018). https://developers.google.com/machine-learning/rules-of-ml/?utm_source=google-ai&utm_medium=card-image&utm_campaign=training-hub&utm_content=ml-rules

Density Estimation in Representation Space to Predict Model Uncertainty

Tiago Ramalho[1] and Miguel Miranda[2(✉)]

[1] Cogent Labs, Tokyo, Japan
`tramalho@cogent.co.jp`
[2] Apple Inc., Cupertino, USA
`miguelnmiranda@apple.com`

Abstract. Deep learning models frequently make incorrect predictions with high confidence when presented with test examples that are not well represented in their training dataset. We propose a novel and straightforward approach to estimate prediction uncertainty in a pre-trained neural network model. Our method estimates the training data density in representation space for a novel input. A neural network model then uses this information to determine whether we expect the pre-trained model to make a correct prediction. This uncertainty model is trained by predicting in-distribution errors, but can detect out-of-distribution data without having seen any such example. We test our method for a state-of-the art image classification model in the settings of both in-distribution uncertainty estimation as well as out-of-distribution detection.

Keywords: Uncertainty estimation · Out of distribution detection

1 Introduction

Deep learning methods have delivered state-of-the art accuracy in challenging tasks such as image classification, language translation, voice-to-speech or learning to act in complex environments. Yet these methods can make incorrect confident predictions when shown certain data [1,22]. As an example consider a deep convolutional networks [14] for image classification are trained with a fixed set of target labels. When shown an image with a class label missing from the original set, the model will (often confidently) predict one of the classes in the training set even though none of them are correct.

At the heart of this issue is the fact that we train models to map a certain data probability distribution to a fixed set of classes. In the real world these models must cope with inputs which fall out of the training distribution. This can be either due to adversarial manipulation [2,12]; drifts in the data distribution or unknown classes.

This kind of uncertainty in the inference result, also known as epistemic uncertainty, cannot be reduced even as the size of the training set increases

© Springer Nature Switzerland AG 2020
O. Shehory et al. (Eds.): EDSMLS 2020, CCIS 1272, pp. 84–96, 2020.
https://doi.org/10.1007/978-3-030-62144-5_7

[24, 28]. To address epistemic uncertainty is is therefore necessary to add a prior to the model which allows for the existence of out-of-distribution data.

In this work we aim to add such a prior by estimating the distance in representation space between a new test point and its closest neighbors in the training set. If the model under consideration is well fit to the training dataset, we expect that distance in a high level representation space will correlate well with distance in the distributional sense. In the following section, we test this hypothesis empirically for the ImageNet dataset and verify that it holds true.

Based on this hypothesis, we propose training a neural network model which takes in as inputs the statistics of a point's neighborhood in representation space, and outputs the probability that the original inference model will make a mistake. This model can be trained using only the original model's training dataset and does not need to train on a separate validation or out-of-distribution dataset.

We compare this method with naive density estimates using a point's nearest neighbors in representation space, as well as with baseline methods such as the predictive uncertainty after the softmax layer and a method based on building gaussian estimates of each class' density. Our method outperforms these baselines and shows a way forward to integrate uncertainty estimates into existing deep neural network models with minor architectural modifications.

In short, the main contributions of this paper are:

- We show that a neural network classification model trained on Imagenet has higher accuracy when the representation of a new data point is close to previously seen representations of that same class. This holds true even for incorrectly classified examples in the training set.
- We use the above observation to propose a simple method to detect out-of-distribution data as well as misclassifications for existing trained models. Crucially, this method does not need to be trained with an external out-of-distribution dataset.
- We test the performance of our method in the challenging scenario of Imagenet image classification and show that it outperforms several baselines. Out-of-distribution prediction is tested on several datasets including Imagenet classes outside of the ILSCVR2012 set, Imagenet-C, and Imagenet-V2.

2   Representation Space in Classification Models

Consider a dataset with N labeled pairs x_i, y_i with x_i usually a high dimensional data element and y_i a lower dimensional label. We wish to train a model to minimize the error in the estimator $\mathrm{argmax}_y P_\theta(y|x)$, with P_θ the probability distribution for the labels output by the model.

This is done by minimizing the cross-entropy between P_θ and the true distribution P of *the training data*. This loss is minimized for points drawn from $P_{\mathrm{train}}(x)$, the training data distribution. We expect a model to generalize well when the support of $P_{\mathrm{test}}(x)$ matches that of $P_{\mathrm{train}}(x)$.

Most interesting datasets are very high dimensional, which makes a direct approximation of the training distribution density computationally challenging.

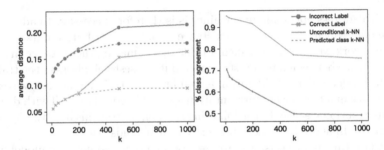

Fig. 1. Quantifying the neighborhood statistics (ILSVRC2012 validation set) of the representation space of the last layer for Inception-ResNet-v2 [30]. We plot the average distance Eq. 1, 2 (left); and class label agreement Eq. 3 (right) between a new representation and its nearest neighbors in the training set conditioned on whether that point was correctly or incorrectly classified. Incorrectly classified data are both further away from their closest neighbors and their predicted labels disagree more with the target prediction.

To alleviate this problem we propose performing the estimation procedure in the high-level representation space used by a neural network model, which can be seen as a compressed representation of the data.

A typical deep neural network model with N layers will transform x via a series of nonlinear maps $r_i = f^i(r_{i-1})$ (with $r_0 = x$). A linear mapping is then applied to the final representation r to obtain the logits $\ell = f^N(r_{N-1})$, which when passed through the softmax function are taken to be an estimate of the class conditional probability distribution $P(y|x)$.

These representations r_i are lower dimensional than x and in particular the last representation r_N in a trained model will have a high mutual information with the variable y (as the posterior $P(y|x)$ is just a linear function of r_N). Therefore, in this space we expect data points with similar classes to roughly cluster together which makes it feasible to use k-nearest neighbors in this space to calculate an approximation of the training set density.

To verify this assumption, we can calculate several summary statistics on the representation space generated by applying a fully trained Inception-ResNet-v2 model [30] to the ImageNet ILSVRC2012 dataset [27].

Let r_i be the representation of input x_i; y_i be its corresponding ground truth label and $\hat{y}_i$ the model's prediction for the class label. Define $\mathcal{N}(r_i, k)$ as set of k-nearest neighbors of r_i. Then, we define the following statistics calculated on the k-nearest neighbors of point x_i:

The unconditional kernel density estimate of x_i with representation r_i

$$P(x_i) \propto \sum_{j \in \mathcal{N}(r_i)}^{k} d(r_i, r_j) \tag{1}$$

with d a suitable kernel (such as the ℓ_2 norm or the cosine similarity) (Fig. 2).

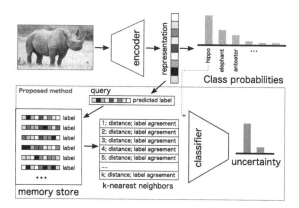

Fig. 2. Schematic of the proposed model for uncertainty estimation. Top row, a deep neural network model is trained using the standard cross-entropy loss to produce class probabilities within a known set. The high level representation (before the logits layer) is additionally stored in a queriable memory database. When a new input is classified, its representation can be used to query the database, and information about its nearest neighbors is fed to the uncertainty model, which predicts the likelihood of the classification result being incorrect.

The class conditional kernel density estimate, which considers only neighbors with the same class as that predicted by the model:

$$P(x_i|\hat{y}_i) \propto \sum_{j \in \mathcal{N}(r_i):\, y_j = y}^{k} d(r_i, r_j) \qquad (2)$$

And the binary agreement density estimate of x_i, which does not use distance information in representation space, but instead counts how many neighbors match the predicted label $\hat{y}$:

$$P(x_i|\hat{y}_i) \propto \sum_{j \in \mathcal{N}(r_i):\, y_j = y}^{k} \mathbb{I}\,(y_j = \hat{y}_i) \qquad (3)$$

This is equivalent to calculating an unweighted kernel density estimate in a ball of radius ϵ with $\epsilon = \max\,(d(r_i, r_j))$. While this is a high variance estimate of $P(x|y)$, it is computationally efficient especially if we are computing an estimate of Eq. 1 at the same time.

We plot the three statistics defined above as a function of k in Fig. 1. We use as test points the images in the validation set, and query the representations of the whole training set to compute the statistics. As hypothesized, points where the network makes a misclassification are significantly more distant than their nearest neighbors, and their neighbors' ground truth labels tend to disagree more with the network's predicted label. The distances for the class-conditional KDE grow more slowly as the effective number of neighbors gets smaller with increasing k.

3   Method

Motivated by the observations above, we wish to propose a method which can use this information to determine whether a new test point is likely to be close to the training data distribution. While the above statistics could be used directly, the density of the training set in the representation space is unlikely to be linearly correlated to the final accuracy of the model. Indeed, in the results section we show that these statistics used directly as an uncertainty measure do not offer as good performance as the model proposed below.

Formally we are looking for a model which can output an uncertainty score given the neighborhood information:

$$u(x_i) = g_\theta(\{(r_j, \mathbb{I}(y_j = \hat{y}_i)\}_{j \in \mathcal{N}(r_i)}, s(\hat{y}_i)) \tag{4}$$

with $s(\hat{y}_i)$ the original model's posterior probability of the predicted label $\hat{y}_i$.

We propose implementing g_θ as a feedforward neural network in order to be able to capture any nonlinear interactions. Furthermore, we want to learn the parameters θ of this model without resorting to any out-of-distribution information. To achieve this we will rely on the related task of detecting a model's mistakes to train the model. This task only requires in-distribution data where the model still makes some mistakes.

We can therefore use either a subset of the validation set or the training set itself as long as the model has not been trained to reach 0% training error. This assumption is often true on state-of-the art models as they are trained with some form of regularization (weight decay, early stopping, etc.). In this case, the mistakes will be data points that are harder to fit as they are more likely to be outliers far from the majority of data.

In this dataset we minimize the binary cross entropy loss

$$\mathcal{L}[u, t] = -t_i \log(u(x_i)) \tag{5}$$

with the binary labels $t_i = 1$ if $y_i = \hat{y}_i$ and $t_i = 0$ otherwise.

As the order with which the model is presented with its inputs should not vary, we use an architecture invariant to permutations in the inputs via the use of an aggregation step [6,32]. g_θ is a model with L layers, where each hidden layer is of the form

$$h_i^l = \sum_{j \in \mathcal{N}(r_i)}^{k} q^l(h_j^{l-1}) \tag{6}$$

where q is a linear transform. For $l > 1$, a nonlinearity is applied to the hidden representation after the aggregation. In this case $L = 1$ corresponds to a linear model. At the very last layer $l = L$ a linear layer with output dimensionality 2 is applied to the aggregated representation to obtain the classification logits.

For the remainder of this paper we will address our proposed method as Neighborhood Uncertainty Classifier (**NUC**). The full training procedure is summarized in Algorithm 1. The algorithm requires a trained model f which returns unnormalized log-probabilities for $\hat{y}$; a precomputed index of all representations at the final layer which we denote by $\mathcal{A}$ for all points in the training set; and the choice of hyperparameter k, the number of nearest neighbors.

For every point in the dataset we obtain the representation and query its k nearest neighbors (excluding the exact point, which will be in the index too). This gives us the set of all neighbor representations as well as their ground truth labels $\{(r_j, y_j)\}$. This information is fed to the model g as well as the predicted class's confidence $s(\hat{y}_i)$ and used to perform one step of gradient descent.

Algorithm 1 NUC training procedure

---

input k number of neighbors, $\mathcal{A}$ the set of all representations, θ model parameters, f
    a trained model
1: **for** epoch $\in$ number of epochs **do**
2:   **for** $x_i \in$ training set **do**
3:     $r_i \leftarrow f^{N-1}(x_i)$
4:     $\hat{y}_i \leftarrow \text{argmax } f^N(r_i)$
5:     $t \leftarrow (y_i == \hat{y}_i)$
6:     $\{(r_j, y_j)\}_{j \in \mathcal{N}(r_i)} \leftarrow \text{knn}(r_i, k, \mathcal{A})$
7:     $u(x_i) \leftarrow g_\theta(\{(r_j, \mathbb{I}(y_j = \hat{y}_i)\}_{j \in \mathcal{N}(r_i)}, s(\hat{y}_i))$
8:     $\theta_{t+1} \leftarrow \theta_t + \lambda \nabla_\theta \mathcal{L}[u(x_i), t]$
9:   **end for**
10: **end for**

---

4 Experiments

We consider two scenarios where the proposed method could be useful: in-distribution uncertainty estimation (i.e. predict incorrect classifications); and out-of-distribution detection. We wish to perform these tests on a real world dataset of practical use, and we therefore choose the widely used Imagenet ILSVRC2012 set. Unlike datasets such as MNIST or CIFAR-10 where performance is saturated [17] and any differences between methods are difficult to see, for ILSVRC2012 there is a lot of headroom to demonstrate the difference between different performing methods.

To generate representations, we use a pretrained checkpoint for the Inception-ResNet-v2 network [30] as it comes close to state of the art accuracy on this dataset and is very widely accessible. The 1.2 million 1536-dimensional vectors needed to represent the whole training set require 5 GB of memory which allows us to keep the complete index in memory in a modern workstation.

We then train the model described in Sect. 3 with $L = 2$ by following the procedure in Algorithm 1 using the Adam optimizer with a learning rate of 10^{-3} annealed to 10^{-4} after 40000 steps. We train the model for one single epoch before testing.

We calculate the performance of all models by a series of threshold-independent measures: the AUROC, AUPR-In and AUPR-Out, as suggested in [11]. For NUC, we take the softmax confidence that the model will make a mistake as the input to the threshold-independent metrics.

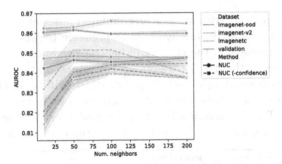

Fig. 3. NUC performance as a function of number of neighbors k. Without taking the softmax prediction confidence into account, the model's performance is strongly dependent on k, as expected. For large values of k the performance slightly degrades as neighbors from potentially very far regions are being taken into account. The full model's performance, however, is relatively constant throughout different values of k.

In Fig. 3 we plot NUC's AUROC as a function of the hyperparameter k. We observe that the method's performance is relatively constant for most values of k. If NUC does not have access to the original model's confidence, however, the performance becomes strongly sensitive on k. This would be expected, as in this case all the inputs of the model depend on the neighborhood information. We can even observe a degradation in performance for very large values of k, as the neighborhood grows more sparse and neighbors from farther away regions are collected. This is consistent with the observations in Fig. 1.

This issue is fixed in the full model, which shows better and more stable performance as it has access to two uncorrelated sources of information. Detailed dataset comparisons are provided in the following section.

4.1 In-Distribution Uncertainty Detection Results

For this task, we use datasets with images following the same distribution as that of the original ILSVRC2012 training set: the ILSVRC2012 validation set; Imagenet-V2 [26], an alternative validation set with subtle distributional shifts (we use the *MatchedFrequency* subset as that is the most challenging); and the Imagenet-C [10] dataset which adds a number of visual perturbations to the images which leave the class unchanged to a human observer.

We use the following methods as comparative baselines: the softmax confidence (both original model's and calibrated confidence on the validation set as in [7]); the kernel density estimates Eq. 1 (average distances), Eq. 3 (neighborhood agreement), Eq. 2 (conditional distances) using 200 k-nearest neighbors; and the mahalanobis distance to the predicted class's centroid (calculated following [17]).

We report results in Table 1. In the case of misclassification prediction for the Imagenet validation dataset NUC beats all the baselines. We note that pure distance based methods don't fare as well as the softmax confidence, possibly because the test points are still close to the training set and misclassifications

Table 1. Results for the in-distribution uncertainty quantification task. We predict classification mistakes (top-1) for the ILSVRC2012 validation set, Imagenet-V2 [26] new validation set and the Imagenet-C [10] dataset. We report the threshold independent metrics AUROC, AUPR-Out and AUPR-In [11]. Items marked with [†] used the calibration procedure described in [7].

	ILSVRC2012$_{valid.}$	Imagenet-V2 [26]	Imagenet-C [10]
	AUROC/AUPR-Out/AUPR-In		
Softmax	0.844/0.587/0.945	0.826/0.682/0.896	0.848/0.812/0.852
Softmax[†]	0.848/0.590/0.948	0.829/0.681/0.899	0.849/0.811/0.854
Equation 1	0.772/0.389/0.930	0.781/0.525/0.893	0.826/0.730/0.862
Equation 2	0.773/0.398/0.931	0.781/0.541/0.892	0.829/0.743/0.865
Equation 3	0.818/0.470/0.950	0.815/0.602/0.914	0.844/0.759/0.883
Mahalanobis	0.786/0.462/0.931	0.798/0.608/0.896	0.842/0.789/0.869
NUC	**0.862/0.600/0.959**	**0.845/0.690/0.923**	**0.862/0.820/0.889**

come from the model not being able to distinguish the data rather than data points finding themselves in unusual places in representation space.

Our method also outperforms other baselines for the Imagenet-V2 and Imagenet-C datasets, which can be considered in-distribution (as they are images containing the same classes as found on the original ILSVRC2012 class set).

4.2   Out-of-Distribution Detection Results

Table 2. Results for the out-of-distribution detection task. The in-distribution set is composed of correctly classified ILSVRC2012 validation set images, and as out-of-distribution sets we consider the following: Imagenet images with unknown classes (details in main text); SVHN [21]; CIFAR-10. We report the threshold independent metrics AUROC, AUPR-Out and AUPR-In [11]. Items marked with [†] used the calibration procedure described in [7].

	Imagenet$_{unk.}$	SVHN [21]	CIFAR-10
	AUROC/AUPR-Out/AUPR-In		
Softmax	0.818/0.832/0.767	0.938/0.948/0.912	0.974/**0.984**/0.945
Softmax[†]	0.821/0.831/0.773	0.938/0.948/0.916	0.975/**0.984**/0.947
Equation 1	0.816/0.767/0.812	0.932/0.896/0.922	0.952/0.863/0.924
Equation 2	0.816/0.771/0.812	0.932/0.899/0.923	0.946/0.838/0.922
Equation 3	0.822/0.786/0.841	0.927/0.890/0.931	0.943/0.794/0.938
Mahalanobis	0.835/0.833/0.817	0.906/0.948/0.814	0.908/0.950/0.813
NUC	**0.846/0.846/0.830**	**0.948/0.953/0.942**	**0.976**/0.979/**0.958**

To test our model in the out-of distribution case we collected 30000 images from the Imagenet database with classes not represented in the original ILSVRC2012 competition's 1000 classes, which we call Imagenet$_{unk.}$. All out-of-distribution datasets are combined with the ILSVRC2012 validation set for positive samples. We also test the model against the SVHN and CIFAR-10 datasets. We report the same metrics as before on all the baselines (Table 2).

For the Imagenet$_{unk.}$ dataset NUC significantly outperforms all other baselines. We note that in this case all distance based methods perform well, and especially the previously proposed Mahalanobis distance-based method beats both softmax and naive nearest neighbors based approaches. These results strengthen our confidence that representation space distance-based approaches can be a valuable tool to detect uncertainty.

In the case of SVHN and CIFAR-10, the performance of other methods is quite robust and therefore the results are all close. As before, NUC provides the best overall performance.

5   Related Work

Existing methods for classification using deep neural networks deliver high accuracy, but suffer from overly-confident outputs and fragility to out-of-distribution data. While ideally we should work towards model architectures which have a built-in concept of uncertainty, here we focus on the more tractable problem of adding uncertainty estimates to the uncertainty unaware model classes currently in widespread use.

The class probabilities output at the softmax layer level can be seen as a baseline for a model's confidence [11]. However, [7] show that powerful models tend to be over-confident in their predictions. This can be measured by calculating whether the empirical accuracy on the test set matches the accuracy estimate implied by the model's confidence. Adjusting the temperature of the softmax function can be used to improve calibration [18].

Further approaches to out-of-distribution detection can be broken down into two categories: either the goal is to calibrate a model's posterior predictive distribution so that out-of-distribution data results in a uniform posterior [8]; or a secondary procedure is developed which produces an uncertainty estimate separate from the model prediction [19,23].

A number of publications focused on steering the network's outputs towards a more uniform distribution in cases where the output is uncertain [15,16]. The idea is that such methods would produce more calibrated confidence estimates as well as uncertainty estimates indirectly derived from the entropy of the confidence distribution.

It is also possible to train a network to predict how certain the original model is by allowing the network to scale the loss function with a predicted uncertainty value, thereby being penalized less for making mistakes for more challenging data [3]. Similarly to our approach, the result is a second model which predicts the uncertainty of the original. In this case the knowledge about uncertainty is implicitly encoded in the auxiliary network's weights rather than in the density of the training data itself.

A number of prior works have used the idea of measuring the distance from a sample to the data manifold to estimate uncertainty. In [4] a kernel density estimate of the likelihood of the current point is fed as a feature along with a dropout uncertainty estimate calculated (as in [5]) to a classifier which can predict adversarial examples reliably.

A number of recent papers used conformal methods to determine what is the probability of a new point being within the data distribution we have observed before. [9] builds class-conditional uncertainty estimates using a kernel density estimator for $P(x|y)$. In [25] the conformal framework is also used, but this time the neighborhood agreement across multiple layers is calculated and aggregated to compute a p-value. This value is used as a proxy for uncertainty.

[13] uses the ratio of the distance between the closest points of the predicted class and the next closest class as a proxy for uncertainty. [17] calculates a class conditional gaussian approximation for $P(x|y)$ in representation space.

A generative model trained on the full data distribution can be used to assess the likelihood of the current test point directly. Such methods have been used in adversarial example detection [31]. Unfortunately current generative models are not yet ready for epistemic uncertainty estimation [20], as they can assign higher likelihoods to out-of-distribution data than to in-distribution. Further research will be necessary to determine how to deploy them in this scenario.

6   Conclusions

In this paper we introduced a new method to detect out-of-distribution data shown to an already trained deep learning model. We proposed training a neural network model which takes in as inputs the statistics of a point's neighborhood in representation space, and outputs the probability that the original inference model will make a mistake. This model can be trained using only the original model's training dataset and does not need to train on a separate validation or out-of-distribution dataset. In this way it can generalize better to out-of-distribution examples, as it only has access to invariant properties of the representation space.

We tested the performance of our method in the challenging scenario of ImageNet image classification and showed that it outperforms several baselines. Both for in-distribution data (ILSCVR2012 set, ImageNet-C, and ImageNet-V2) and out-of-distribution data (ImageNet new classes, CIFAR10, SVHN), NUC beats all baselines under comparison.

An improvement outside of the scope of this work would be to find a minimal set of support neighbors (similar to Prototype Networks [29]) which can be queried instead of the full training set. We expect distance-based methods such as the one here suggested can be further improved and be used a general tool to introduce uncertainty in deep neural networks.

Acknowledgements. The authors thank Elco Bakker for insightful feedback and comments on the paper.

A   Appendix

We tuned the hyperparameters L, the number of layers; and k the number of nearest numbers fed to the classifier. All models were trained using the Adam optimizer with a learning rate of 10^{-3} annealed to 10^{-4} after 40000 steps. We train each model for one single epoch before validating. We considered the following values for hyperparameters: $L \in [1, 2, 3]$ (with $L = 1$ corresponding to a linear model) and $k \in [10, 50, 100, 200]$.

We chose the hyperparameters used in the paper $L = 2, k = [10, 200]$ based on the AUROC [11] on the in-distribution mistake prediction task using the ILSVRC2012 validation set (Fig. 4).

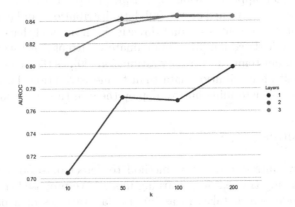

Fig. 4. AUROC metric reported for models with $L \in [1, 2, 3]$ and $k \in [10, 50, 100, 200]$.

References

1. Amodei, D., Olah, C., Steinhardt, J., Christiano, P., Schulman, J., Mané, D.: Concrete problems in AI safety. arXiv:1606.06565 [cs], June 2016
2. Athalye, A., Engstrom, L., Ilyas, A., Kwok, K.: Synthesizing robust adversarial examples. arXiv:1707.07397 [cs], July 2017
3. DeVries, T. and Taylor, G.W.: Learning confidence for out-of-distribution detection in neural networks. arXiv:1802.04865 [cs, stat], February 2018
4. Feinman, R., Curtin, R.R., Shintre, S., Gardner, A.B.: Detecting adversarial samples from artifacts. arXiv:1703.00410 [cs, stat], March 2017
5. Gal, Y., Ghahramani, Z.: Dropout as a Bayesian approximation: representing model uncertainty in deep learning. arXiv:1506.02142 [cs, stat], June 2015
6. Garnelo, M., et al.: Conditional neural processes. arXiv:1807.01613 [cs, stat], July 2018

7. Guo, C., Pleiss, G., Sun, Y., Weinberger, K.Q.: On calibration of modern neural networks. arXiv:1706.04599 [cs], June 2017
8. Hafner, D., Tran, D., Lillicrap, T., Irpan, A., Davidson, J.: Reliable uncertainty estimates in deep neural networks using noise contrastive priors. arXiv preprint arXiv:1807.09289 (2018)
9. Hechtlinger, Y., Póczos, B., Wasserman, L.: Cautious deep learning. arXiv:1805.09460 [cs, stat], May 2018
10. Hendrycks, D., Dietterich, T.: Benchmarking neural network robustness to common corruptions and perturbations. arXiv:1903.12261 [cs, stat], March 2019
11. Hendrycks, D., Gimpel, K.: A baseline for detecting misclassified and out-of-distribution examples in neural networks. arXiv:1610.02136 [cs], October 2016
12. Huang, S., Papernot, N., Goodfellow, I., Duan, Y., Abbeel, P.: Adversarial attacks on neural network policies (2017)
13. Jiang, H., Kim, B., Guan, M., Gupta, M.: To trust or not to trust a classifier. arXiv:1805.11783 [cs, stat], May 2018
14. Krizhevsky, A., Sutskever, I., Hinton, G.E.: Imagenet classification with deep convolutional neural networks. In: Advances in Neural Information Processing Systems, pp. 1097–1105 (2012)
15. Lakshminarayanan, B., Pritzel, A., Blundell, C.: Simple and scalable predictive uncertainty estimation using deep ensembles. In: Advances in Neural Information Processing Systems, pp. 6402–6413 (2017)
16. Lee, K., Lee, H., Lee, K., Shin, J.: Training confidence-calibrated classifiers for detecting out-of-distribution samples. arXiv:1711.09325 [cs, stat], November 2017
17. Lee, K., Lee, K., Lee, H., Shin, J.: A simple unified framework for detecting out-of-distribution samples and adversarial attacks. arXiv:1807.03888 [cs, stat], July 2018
18. Liang, S., Li, Y., Srikant, R.: Enhancing the reliability of out-of-distribution image detection in neural networks. arXiv:1706.02690 [cs, stat], June 2017
19. Malinin, A., Gales, M.: Predictive uncertainty estimation via prior networks. In: Advances in Neural Information Processing Systems, pp. 7047–7058 (2018)
20. Nalisnick, E., Matsukawa, A., Teh, Y.W., Gorur, D., Lakshminarayanan, B.: Do deep generative models know what they don't know? arXiv:1810.09136 [cs, stat], October 2018
21. Netzer, Y., Wang, T., Coates, A., Bissacco, A., Wu, B., Ng, A.Y.: Reading digits in natural images with unsupervised feature learning. In: NIPS Workshop on Deep Learning and Unsupervised Feature Learning 2011 (2011)
22. Nguyen, A., Yosinski, J., Clune, J.: Deep neural networks are easily fooled: high confidence predictions for unrecognizable images, December 2014
23. Oberdiek, P., Rottmann, M., Gottschalk, H.: Classification uncertainty of deep neural networks based on gradient information. arXiv:1805.08440 [cs, stat], May 2018
24. Osband, I., Aslanides, J., Cassirer, A.: Randomized prior functions for deep reinforcement learning. arXiv:1806.03335 [cs, stat], June 2018
25. Papernot, N., McDaniel, P.: Deep k-nearest neighbors: towards confident, interpretable and robust deep learning, March 2018
26. Recht, B., Roelofs, R., Schmidt, L., Shankar, V.: Do imagenet classifiers generalize to imagenet? arXiv preprint arXiv:1902.10811 (2019)
27. Russakovsky, O., et al.: ImageNet large scale visual recognition challenge. Int. J. Comput. Vis. **115**(3), 211–252 (2015). https://doi.org/10.1007/s11263-015-0816-y

28. Sensoy, M., Kaplan, L., Kandemir, M.: Evidential deep learning to quantify classi-fication uncertainty. In: Advances in Neural Information Processing Systems, pp. 3179–3189 (2018)
29. Snell, J., Swersky, K., Zemel, R.: Prototypical networks for few-shot learning. arXiv:1703.05175 [cs, stat], March 2017
30. Szegedy, C., Ioffe, S., Vanhoucke, V., Alemi, A.: Inception-v4, Inception-ResNet and the impact of residual connections on learning, February 2016
31. Uesato, J., O'Donoghue, B., Oord, A.V.D., Kohli, P.: Adversarial risk and the dangers of evaluating against weak attacks. arXiv:1802.05666 [cs, stat], February 2018
32. Zaheer, M., Kottur, S., Ravanbakhsh, S., Poczos, B., Salakhutdinov, R.R., Smola, A.J.: Deep sets. arXiv:1703.06114 [cs, stat], March 2017

Automated Detection of Drift in Deep Learning Based Classifiers Performance Using Network Embeddings

Parijat Dube[1] and Eitan Farchi[2(✉)]

[1] IBM Research, New York, USA
pdube@us.ibm.com
[2] IBM Research, Haifa, Israel
farchi@il.ibm.com

Abstract. In supervised learning, neural network generalize, or learn, based on various statistical properties of the training data. Typically, an unseen randomly sampled test set is used to estimate the performance (e.g., accuracy) of the neural network during deployment time. The performance on the test set is used to project the performance of the neural network at deployment time under the implicit assumption that the data distribution of the test set represents the data distribution at deployment time.

This assumption often breaks in real world deployment scenarios. Statistic characteristics of the data may change between training time and deployment time. For example, new unforeseen objects may emerge in the data, the data may become noisy due to external conditions (e.g., rain), or characteristic of objects may change over time (e.g., subjects with a new group age). All of these changes in the data, may degrade the performance of the neural network below an anticipated and desired threshold. However, if the production data is not labeled, as is typically the case in deployment time, detection of such a drift in network performance is not straightforward. We develop a technique that identifies drift in neural network performance in time windows for which the data is not labeled. We take advantage of the network structure, specifically the vector of activation level at the layer before the last for a given data point x, to define the statistic used to identify drift. We use cosine similarity as statistics defined on the vector of activation level at the layer before the last. We then apply non-parametric statistical tests on a sliding window of the time series of data arrivals to identify drift. The approach efficiently detects drift and is only sensitive to the choice of the sliding window which needs to have sufficient overlap with the window in which the drift is gradually introduced.

Keywords: Deep learning · Drift detection · Embeddings · Divergence

© Springer Nature Switzerland AG 2020
O. Shehory et al. (Eds.): EDSMLS 2020, CCIS 1272, pp. 97–109, 2020.
https://doi.org/10.1007/978-3-030-62144-5_8

1   Introduction

This paper addresses the issue of detecting when the performance, such as accuracy, of a neural network becomes unacceptable due to the introduction of new class of objects the network was not trained on. We assume that the identification should be done when the system is already deployed and the data is not labeled. For example, assume the neural network was trained to detect different types of weapons, implicitly assuming only weapons will be analyzed, and during deployment it is presented with images of tools as well. Since images at deployment time are not labeled as weapons and tools there is no easy way to detect drift in the network performance. This drift in performance is due to introduction of images belonging to a new class, which was not present in the training dataset. Yet as another example consider a model trained to detect images of a cell phone prior to the introduction of smart phones. Even if the model had 100% accuracy, it would perform miserably on modern day images where virtually all cellphones are smart phones with a huge screen and no keyboard! Obviously, the transition from dumb phones to smart phones was gradual, and one would like to know that the neural network is performing poorly as early as possible.

The neural network makes statistical assumptions in order to generalize or 'learn' from training data. Often, the statistical characteristics of the data change between training time and deployment time. These changes may or may not affect the neural network performance. For example, if the accuracy of the classifier is the same on each label a shift in the percentage of labels of a certain type, e.g., percentage of cats, in a time window will not impact the overall performance of the neural network although the distribution of data has changed. On the other hand, if the accuracy of the neural network is different on dogs and cats then a change in the distribution of cats will affect the overall performance of the neural network.

We refer to the gradual change in input data that impacts the neural network performance as *Data Drift*, and claim that detection of such drift is a significant aspect of the network quality. We take after [11] but specifically assume that we are dealing with a neural network and explore its inner structure to detect the drift. Specially, we consider the layer before the last of the neural network as it was shown [16] that higher layers in the network typically best represent the abstractions created by the network. Also, recent advances in readability of neural networks [12] attributed a relevance measure to each neuron thus succeeding in explaining the reason for a classification of a specific data point. We are following this idea and attempting to use the activation value in each neuron to analyze drift.

We use the vector of activation values at the neurons of the network's layer before the last layer (i.e., the layer before the softmax output layer). We use this vector to define statistics that detect the drift. Specifically, the similarity between these vectors is a measure of divergence in the embedding space. Details of the approach are provided in the methodology section.

One may be tempted to directly identify a drift in the data distribution using standard density estimation techniques. As indicated above, having a distribution divergence may not necessarily result in a drift in the neural network performance. In addition, the challenge of distribution drift identification is a well-acknowledged one, for example underlying much of the Bayesian networks work. Density estimation is largely unfeasible because of the high dimensionality of the data, though there are attempts to make progress on that front (see section on related work).

Another practical approach to the problem is to require sampling and manual labeling data at deployment time. Frequently comparing production output to true labels may be unfeasible. Labeling may be expensive, experts that are able to label the input may be unavailable, and during production labeling is frequently delayed, which may be intolerable.

We note that while there is substantial experience in developing successful ML solutions in areas where there is a lot of labeled training data, labeling is cheap, and only light domain knowledge is required, less experience exists in developing successful ML solutions when any of these conditions break. However, these conditions often break in the domain of business applications making the drift problem important.

The main contributions of this work are:

1. An algorithm to detect drift in performance of a neural network that takes advantage of the internal structure of the network.
2. An analysis of the performance of our proposed technique by calculating detection delay and false alarms in 15 different image classification scenarios with data drift.

The methodology section introduces our drift detection technique and algorithm. We then report our simulation results of gradually introducing new objects and detecting drift. We analyze the efficacy of the approach in the experimental section. We then discussed related work and conclude.

2 Methodology

We first describe an approach to calculate divergence between two data sets. For any two datasets A and B, a divergence vector $\mathcal{D}_{AB}$ is defined as a vector whose elements are a measure of divergence in the feature space between the average feature vectors of objects in the the two datasets. Let A be a dataset and let M be a Deep Neural Network (DNN) with N convolutional layers. Then for each image $a \in A$ we obtain feature vector for a convolution layer in M by doing a forward pass of the image. Let $f_{a,n}$ be the feature vector of object a from layer n, where $n = 1, \ldots, N$. For our analysis, we assume that the activation values are non-negative. This is true for certain activation functions, e.g., ReLU (the most common activation function for inner layers) or can be achieved by applying appropriate thresholding to activation values. Next calculate the average feature vector f_n^A of A for layer n as:

$$f_n^A = \frac{1}{|A|} \sum_{a \in A} f_{a,n},$$

where $|A|$ is the cardinality of A. Observe that f_n^A is a vector of dimension d_n, the number of activations of layer n. Similarly we obtain f_n^B. Let $\mathcal{D}_{AB}$ be the layerwise divergence between datasets A and B. Thus $\mathcal{D}_{AB}$ is an N-dimension vector, with the nth element, $\mathcal{D}_{AB,n}$ being a divergence between the average feature vectors f_n^A and f_n^B. To calculate $\mathcal{D}_{AB}$ different measures to measure the similarity between vectors can be used like cosine similarity and Kullback-Leibler (KL) divergence [7]. The cosine similarity between the two vectors f_n^A and f_n^B is given by:

$$cos(f_n^A, f_n^B) = \frac{f_n^A \cdot f_n^B}{\|f_n^A\|\|f_n^B\|}.$$

Observe that for discrete probability distributions, p and q, KL divergence is a measure of the difference between p and q and is defined as

$$KLD(p,q) = \sum_i p(i) log\left(\frac{p(i)}{q(i)}\right).$$

Since KL divergence is defined over probability distributions, we need to appropriately normalize the feature vectors before calculating the KL divergence. A normalized average feature vector $\hat{f}_n^A$ is obtained as follows:

$$\hat{f}_n^A = \frac{f_n^A}{\sum f_n^A}.$$

Observe that all the elements of $\hat{f}_n^A$ sum to 1 and hence qualify as a discrete probability distribution. Then $\mathcal{D}_{AB,n}$ is defined as:

$$\mathcal{D}_{AB,n} = \frac{KLD(\hat{f}_n^A, \hat{f}_n^B) + KLD(\hat{f}_n^B, \hat{f}_n^A)}{2}.$$

We calculate divergence in feature space between objects in production data. If the distribution of divergence calculated using the objects in production data does not exhibit statistical similarity to distribution of divergence using the images in training dataset there is a data drift. This implies that the production data has deviated significantly from training data and therefore classification results may be incorrect. The classifier needs to be retrained with the new class distribution manifested by the production data. This requires adding new class labels (if one or more of the production classes were not present in the training dataset) and then retraining.

We next provide information on the data drift detection algorithm, the data sets and classifier models that we use in our time simulation which gradually introduces a drift.

2.1   The Data Drift Detection Algorithm

To detect change in divergence distribution we use the Mann-Whitney non-parametric test [8,9]. This is a non parametric test that checks if two sampled datasets are from the same distribution or not. This fits our need as we cannot make any assumptions about the distribution of the two samples. Further, we choose the Mann-Whitney test over the t-test as we are not interested in the difference of the mean of the two populations but whether or not the two distributions are indeed different.

In this work we focus on the layer before the last of the network. We thus focus on f_{N-1}^A for a given data set A. The drift detection algorithm is summarized in Algorithm 1. We use consecutive windows to determine if the drift occurred. The drift detection algorithm performs a non-parametric statistical test for the divergence over the consecutive windows. A drift alert is triggered if the distributions are significantly different. The three hyperparameters in the algorithm are $\alpha, \beta,$ and γ. While the value of $\alpha = 0.05$ is a standard choice in statistical control, the value of $\gamma = 5$ gave the best trade-off between detection delay and false alarms. As for β, its value is chosen to get enough samples in the two groups D_1 and D_2.

Algorithm 1: Drift detection algorithm.

Result: DRIFT detected
//Set your significance level
$\alpha = 0.05$;
β = sliding window size;
D_1 = the first $\beta/2$ data points;
D_2 = the second $\beta/2$ data points;
$\gamma = 5$;
//We declare drift after drift was found γ consecutive times
found = 0;
while True do
    //Get the P value form Mann-Whitney test on D_1 and D_2
    $P = Whitney(D_1, D_2)$;
    if $P < \alpha$ **then**
        | found++;
    else
        | found=0;
    end
    if *found* $== \gamma$ **then**
        | report DRIFT;
        | found=0;
    end
    Advance the sliding window.
    Reset D_1 and D_2 by shifting the sliding window.
end

2.2   Data and Classifiers

We present our technique using a specific case study involving images, with datasets created by vertically partitioning ImageNet22K [2] along its nine distinct subtrees: animals, plants, weapon, tool, music, fungus, fruit, garment, and fabric. The 9 datasets and their characteristics are shown in Table 1.

Table 1. Datasets used in our evaluation

Dataset	Images	Classes
animals	2783524	3796
plants	2224816	4040
fabric	159110	232
fruit	185091	307
fungus	135919	299
garment	214172	252
music	137770	156
tool	175095	317
weapon	102946	138

We use these domains to simulate a gradual move from a base distribution to a target distribution that includes objects for which the classifier was not trained on. To achieve that, each of these domains was split into three partitions. First was used to train the baseline model, second was used to validate the baseline, and third was used to introduce drift and move to the target dataset distribution.

In this way, we generated 9 baseline datasets and 9 target datasets. The training of the baseline network was done using Caffe [6] using a ResNet-27 model [5]. The baseline networks were trained for 900,000 iterations with a step size of 300,000 iterations and an initial learning rate of 0.01.

2.3   Experiment Design

A drift scenario is characterized by a change in production data distribution from a baseline distribution to a target distribution over a period of time. The length of time from the onset of drift (when the first object belonging to the target distribution appears in the production data) to the completion of drift (the first time when the production data has all objects belonging to the target distribution) is called the *drift period*. The length of this drift period can vary from very short (say, 1–4 production objects) to very long (several hundred production objects). Further the drift can be abrupt or gradual. Observe that an abrupt drift is like a step change in distribution, whereas a linear drift has a constant rate of increase in the fraction of objects belonging to the target distribution. We can simulate different drift scenarios by varying two associated features:

1. *Baseline and target distribution*: For the experiments we used 15 different combinations of baseline and target datasets using the 9 datasets from Table 1.
2. *Drift function*: Different functions can be used to simulate the pace of drift, e.g., (i) step, (ii) linear, and (iii) exponential.

Each scenario is labeled as a tuple:
$\{<baseline>, <target>, <drift>\}$.

Thus $\{animals, plants, linear\}$ is a scenario where the baseline dataset is animals and the production drifts at a constant rate to plants dataset. To simulate a scenario, we first use the baseline dataset and train a DNN based classifier. This model is assumed to represent the model deployed in production. As long as the production data follows the baseline dataset distribution, the deployed model will be performing well with expected performance. After some time, the drift period starts and the production data start drifting from the baseline dataset distribution. This is achieved by adding objects from the target distribution in the production data with the drift progress governed by the drift function. Over a period of time the fraction of images from the target dataset in the production data keep increasing. We say that the production data has completely drifted (i.e., the drift period has ended) when it only has objects from the target dataset and no objects from the baseline dataset. After the production data has completely drifted, its distribution is same as the target dataset distribution. Our technique will identify the drift before it completely drifted. This is desired as typically, in production, drift will settle on an intermediate state in which the new objects are occurring at some given frequency.

3   Experimental Results

We did experiments with linear drift and evaluated the efficacy of our technique in detecting the data drift. Each experiment starts at time $t_0 = 0$ and simulates a drift scenario, where the drift period starts at t_s and ends at t_e. Between t_s and t_e the data distribution drifts at a constant rate of $\frac{1}{t_e - t_s}$. We ran 15 different experiments with varying combination of baseline and target datasets. Table 2 provides the set of baseline and target datasets used in our experiments. To detect drift we apply the change detection test using Algorithm 1 on the time series of divergence calculated using the cosine similarity. We calculate average feature vector over a set of consecutive images (batch of 3 images) and compare this with average feature vectore of the next batch. The time series of divergence between two consecutive batches is our observation set for change detection.

Observe that, our technique assumes that divergence distribution of datasets is inherently different and can be effectively used to differentiate different datasets and hence identify data drift. We first validate this assumption using empirical data. Figure 1 shows divergence distribution of production data for 4 of the 15 experiments. The drift period is from $t_s = 60$ to $t_e = 80$. The distinction between divergence distribution before and after the drift period is visually evident for all the 4 cases.

Table 2. Evaluation of our drift detection algorithm on 15 drift scenarios. Our algorithm detected drift with an 100% success rate (15/15 cases) with an average detection delay of 23 epochs after the drift is introduced (t_s).

Baseline	Target	Detection	Detection delay	False alarms
animals	plants	Yes	23	1
animals	fruit	Yes	10	2
animals	fungus	Yes	27	1
animals	fabric	Yes	28	0
animals	garment	Yes	29	0
animals	music	Yes	26	0
animals	weapon	Yes	12	0
animals	tool	Yes	27	0
plants	animals	Yes	17	0
plants	fruit	Yes	22	0
plants	fungus	Yes	18	2
music	tool	Yes	23	0
music	weapon	Yes	33	0
music	fabric	Yes	15	0
music	garment	Yes	27	0

We next describe our change detection approach using Mann-Whitney test, specifically we use the *Mann–Whitney U* SciPy Python library. At this point our goal is to check if the change in data distribution manifested as a change in drift distribution can be detected by simple non-parametric approaches. Mann-Whitney test compares samples from two groups and decides whether they belong to the same or different distribution. In our experiments, we assume that production data is coming continuously and a batch of objects in production data constitutes one epoch of observation. At each observation epoch we calculate the divergence between the current batch of images and the batch at the previous epoch. Let this batch size be b_s. Thus, at every observation epoch we generate a new data in the divergence time series. Let β be the window of observation for the Mann-Whitney test. At any observation epoch t we generate two groups, one consisting of observation data (i.e., divergence values) from epoch $t - \beta + 1$ to $t - \beta/2$, call this D_1 and the other consisting of observation data from epoch $t - \beta/2 + 1$ to t, call this D_2. We fix our significance level at 0.05. We obtain a *P-value* associated with Mann-Whitney test using D_1 and D_2 from `scipy.stats.mannwhitneyu`. The test requires independence of observation within each population. Further research will touch on that point. If this *P-value* if smaller than our significance level we conclude that D_1 and D_2 belong to different distributions and hence indicative of data drift. However, if the *P-value* is larger than our chosen significance level we do not have any strong

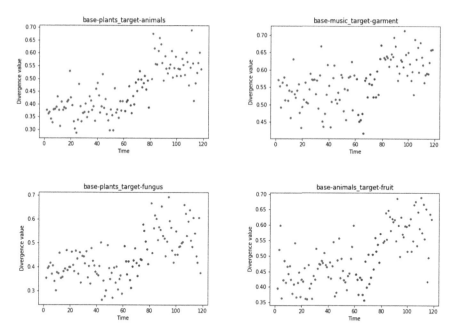

Fig. 1. Inter-batch divergence distribution over the experiment interval for 4 of the 15 scenarios. Each scenario is identified by a combination of base and target distribution. Drift starts at $t = 60$ and ends at $t = 80$. The divergence values before t_s are shown in magenta, during the drift in blue, and after t_e in green. (Color figure online)

indication of change in distribution. Since Mann-Whitney test is less powerful when sample size is small, we take β to be at least 40 in our experiments. This implies that D_1 and D_2 cannot be smaller than 20.

As we consecutively apply the test there is an increased chance of the low probability event represented by our significance level occurring. To correct for that we do not report the drift right away but only after the drift is detected several consecutive epochs by the Mann-Whitney resulting in another hyper parameter (γ in Algorithm 1). This can be further refined using stopping time techniques [3] to avoid the additional hyper parameter.

Assume the time we have identified the drift is t. We define the detection time $t_d = t - t_s$. Figure 2 shows the performance of our drift detection algorithm in 4 of the 15 experimental scenarios with different baseline and target dataset. Our algorithm detected drift with a 100% success rate (15/15 cases) with an average detection delay of 23 epochs after the drift is introduced (t_s) and in all except one case the change was detected before the completion of drift period (t_e).

When a change is detected the algorithm is reset ("found" parameter set to 0) which can cause multiple change detection during the drift period. This resetting helps in continuous monitoring for drift and not just stop after the first detection. Observe that divergence is a measure of similarity of the images in

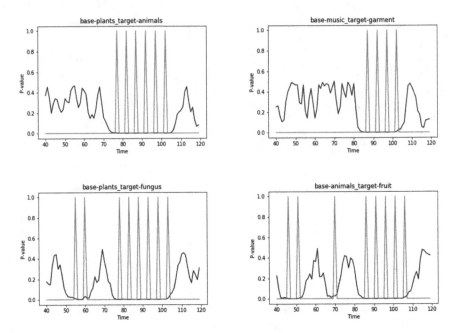

Fig. 2. Drift detection by applying Mann-Whitney test on inter-batch divergence distribution over the experiment interval for 4 of the 15 scenarios. Each scenario is identified by a combination of base and target distribution. Drift starts at $t = 60$ and finishes at $t = 80$. At each epoch calculated P value is shown in green. A drift is detected when consecutively five P values are indicative of difference in distribution. The epoch(s) when the algorithm detects the change are marked by a change in value of red curve from 0 to 1. When a change is detected the algorithm is reset ("found" parameter set to 0) resulting in multiple change detection during the drift period. (Color figure online)

batches. The batch size also affects the robustness of the divergence metric. It will be interesting to understand the sensitivity of algorithm to batch size and γ. From

4   Related Work

In practice one may attempt to determine if the distribution of the data has changed accepting the fact that false alarms may result from identifying distribution changes that are not impacting the network performance. Empirical density estimation has been well investigated and a variety of approaches exist for the classical settings in which the data has low dimensionality or is drawn from a known distribution or mixture of distributions.

It has also been acknowledged that density estimation becomes very challenging for high-dimensional data [13]. Modeling multivariate data with Bayesian networks is one example for a domain that has been struggling with this challenge [15].

Earlier work have proposed high dimensionality density estimation, such as Maximum Mean Discrepancy [4] or Wasserstein distance [10]. However, statistical calculations like a confidence interval, which depend on the distribution, become much more complicated for high dimension metrics than uni-variate metrics. Further, as the dimensionality increases so does the likelihood of having insufficient data for reliably performing such statistical calculations.

In [11] drift detection is attempted using a uni-variate machine learning model confidence interval as a statistics. This work is black box – it applies to any machine learning approach that produces a confidence number but does not take advantage of the inner structure of the machine learning model. In contrast, given the importance of neural networks, we drive new statistics that take advantage of the structure of the network but follow [11] and collapsing the statistic we apply to a uni-variate statistic avoiding thus avoiding the curse of high dimensions incurred when attempting to approximate the distribution directly.

Another approach to the change in data distribution is to increase the robustness of the model so that it better handle changes in the data, identify data missing from the training examples or identify bias in the training examples. Such approaches often focus on handling missing data or direct learning to areas in the data where the model performs poorly. Ensembles of weak learners such as AdaBoost are an example. Further research is needed to analyze the relation between such approaches, distribution drift and model performance drift.

Various work captures challenges and best practices in developing ML solutions, e.g., [1,14,17]. Interestingly model performance drift is not addressed by this work. Our research deals with capturing the expected envelope of operation of a network and monitoring for significant changes against it. The approach is especially important when the production data is not labeled which is the case in many business applications.

5   Conclusion

We examine the problem of network performance drift at deployment time due to the gradual introduction of new objects. We devise an efficient way to detect such drift exploiting the inner structure of the neural network. The method efficiently detects drift in unlabeled production data. The only dependency is that the size of the sliding window should have sufficient overlap with the size of the window in which the change have occurred.

We have demonstrated our approach using 15 scenarios of data drift. In each of these scenarios, we have a baseline data distribution on which the network is trained with and then the production data is gradually drifted to a different distribution. The two distributions have non overlapping class labels. For example, in one scenario, the baseline distribution has images belonging to the animals category and after drift the distribution has images belonging to plants category.

Future work will compare different methods of drift detection and analyze how quickly the method identifies the drift while minimizing false alarms. We will analyze the algorithm under different drift scenarios where the drift is characterized by a change in mixture of the classes in which the class labels before and after drift may have some overlap. Finally, future work will further explore the inner structure of the network, determine if there are best layers to identify the drift from, and explore if the approach we took to drift detection is related to abstraction creates by the network.

References

1. Breck, E., Cai, S., Nielsen, E., Salib, M., Sculley, D.: What's your ml test score? A rubric for ml production systems. In: Reliable Machine Learning in the Wild - NIPS 2016 Workshop (2016)
2. Deng, J. and Dong, W., Socher, R., Li, L.J.L.K., FeiFei, L.: ImageNet: a large-scale hierarchical image database. In: IEEE Conference on CVPR (2009)
3. Egloff, D.: Monte Carlo algorithms for optimal stopping and statistical learning. Ann. Appl. Probab. **15**(2), 1396–1432 (2005). http://www.jstor.org/stable/30038358
4. Gretton, A., Borgwardt, K.M., Rasch, M.J., Schölkopf, B., Smola, A.: A Kernel two-sample test. J. Mach. Learn. Res. **13**, 723–773 (2012). http://dl.acm.org/citation.cfm?id=2188385.2188410
5. He, K., Zhang, X., Ren, S., Sun, J.: Deep residual learning for image recognition. In: IEEE Conference on CVPR (2016)
6. Jia, Y., et al.: Caffe: convolutional architecture for fast feature embedding. In: ACM Multimedia (2014)
7. Kullback, S., Leibler, R.A.: On information and sufficiency. Ann. Math. Statist. **22**(1), 79–86 (1951)
8. Mann, H.B., Whitney, D.R.: On a test of whether one of two random variables is stochastically larger than the other. Ann. Math. Stat. **18**(1), 50–60 (1947)
9. Nachar, N.: The Mann-Whitney U: a test for assessing whether two independent samples come from the same distribution. Tutorials Quant. Methods Psychol. **4**(1), 13–20 (2008)
10. Olkin, I., Pukelsheim, F.: The distance between two random vectors with given dispersion matrices. Linear Algebra Appl. **48**, 257–263 (1982)
11. Raz, O., Zalmanovici, M., Zlotnick, A., Farchi, E.: Automatically detecting data drift in machine learning based classifiers. In: The AAAI-19 Workshop on Engineering Dependable and Secure Machine Learning Systems Software Engineering for Machine Learning (EDSMLS 2019) (2019). https://drive.google.com/file/d/1vPZkZ_s5qky7ua-iDgOQ9St-ruFC8yce/view
12. Samek, W., Wiegand, T., Müller, K.: Explainable artificial intelligence: understanding, visualizing and interpreting deep learning models. CoRR abs/1708.08296 (2017). http://arxiv.org/abs/1708.08296
13. Schölkopf, B., Platt, J.C., Shawe-Taylor, J.C., Smola, A.J., Williamson, R.C.: Estimating the support of a high-dimensional distribution. Neural Comput. **13**(7), 1443–1471 (2001)
14. Sculley, D., et al.: Machine learning: the high interest credit card of technical debt. In: SE4ML: Software Engineering for Machine Learning (NIPS 2014 Workshop) (2014)
15. Smith, J., Croft, J.: Bayesian networks for discrete multivariate data: an algebraic approach to inference. J. Multivar. Anal. **84**(2), 387–402 (2003)

16. Yosinski, J., Clune, J., Bengio, Y., Lipson, H.: How transferable are features in deep neural networks? In: Ghahramani, Z., Welling, M., Cortes, C., Lawrence, N.D., Weinberger, K.Q. (eds.) Advances in Neural Information Processing Systems, vol. 27, pp. 3320–3328. Curran Associates, Inc. (2014)
17. Zinkevich, M.: Rules of machine learning: best practices for ml engineering. Google (2018). https://developers.google.com/machine-learning/rules-of-ml/?utm_source=google-ai&utm_medium=card-image&utm_campaign=training-hub&utm_content=ml-rules

Quality of Syntactic Implication of RL-Based Sentence Summarization

Hoa T. Le[1(✉)], Christophe Cerisara[1,2(✉)], and Claire Gardent[2(✉)]

[1] Laboratory LORIA, Nancy, France
{hoa.le,christophe.cerisara}@loria.fr
[2] CNRS/LORIA, Nancy, France
claire.gardent@loria.fr

Abstract. Work on summarization has explored both reinforcement learning (RL) optimization using ROUGE as a reward and syntax-aware models, such as models whose input is enriched with part-of-speech (POS)-tags and dependency information. However, it is not clear what is the respective impact of these approaches beyond the standard ROUGE evaluation metric. Especially, RL-based for summarization is becoming more and more popular. Using the standard Gigaword sentence summarization task, we compare an RL self-critical sequence training (SCST) method with syntax-aware models that leverage POS tags and Dependency information. We show that on all quantitative and qualitative evaluations, the combined model gives the best results, but also that only training with RL and without any syntactic information already gives nearly as good results as syntax-aware models with less parameters and faster training convergence.

1 Introduction

Early neural approaches to text generation tasks such as machine translation, summarization and image captioning mostly relied on sequence-to-sequence models [24] where the model was trained using cross-entropy and features were learned automatically. More recent work however, shows that using reinforcement learning or explicitly enriching the input with additional linguistic features helps to improve performance.

Reinforcement learning was proposed to address two shortcomings of cross entropy training. First, there is a discrepancy between how the model is trained (conditioned on the ground truth) and used at test time (using argmax or beam search), namely the *exposure bias* problem. Second, the evaluation metrics (for ex. ROUGE, METEOR, BLEU, etc.) differ from the objective that is maximized with the standard cross-entropy on each token; this is known as the *loss mismatch* problem. Typically, RL is used to optimize task-specific objectives such as ROUGE for text summarization systems [5,15–17] and SARI [28] for sentence simplification models [30].

Similarly, while neural networks allow for features to be learned automatically, explicitly enriching the input with linguistic features was repeatedly shown

© Springer Nature Switzerland AG 2020
O. Shehory et al. (Eds.): EDSMLS 2020, CCIS 1272, pp. 110–125, 2020.
https://doi.org/10.1007/978-3-030-62144-5_9

to improve performance. For instance, [12,23] show that adding morphological features, part-of-speech (POS) tags, syntactic dependency and or parse trees as input features improves the performance of neural machine translation (NMT) systems; and [14] that integrating linguistic features such as POS tags and named-entities helps to improve summarization.

In this paper, we explore the relative impact of these two approaches on sentence summarization. More precisely, we assess and compare the quality of the summaries generated by syntax-aware, RL-trained and combined models with regard to several qualitative aspects that strongly impact the perceived quality of the generated texts: number of repetitions, sentence length, distribution of part-of-speech tags, relevance and grammaticality.

Using the standard Gigaword benchmark corpus, we compare and combine an RL self-critical sequence training (SCST) method with syntax-aware models that leverage POS tags and/or dependency information. We show that both enhancements, syntactic information and RL training, benefit to a sequence-to-sequence summarization model with attention and copy-pointer mechanism. While the combined model gives the best quality of summaries, we also show that the reinforcement learning approach alone may be preferred when computational complexity is an issue, as it gives nearly as good results as the syntax-aware model but with less parameters and faster training convergence.

2   Related Work

We briefly discuss previous work on syntax-aware and RL-based models for text-to-text generation focusing on summarization and NMT and we position our work with respect to these approaches.

Syntax Models: Explicit modeling of syntax has frequently been used in text generation applications in particular, for NMT and summarization. Thus [23] enrich the input to NMT with dependency labels, POS tags, subword tags and lemmas so that each input token is represented by the concatenation of word and features embeddings. Similarly, [14] enrich the encoder side of a neural summarization model with POS tag, NER tag, TF-IDF features. The intuition is that words will be better disambiguated by taking syntactic context into account. Speculating that full parse trees can be more beneficial for NMT than shallow syntactic information, [12] enrich the input with a linearization of its parse tree and compares three ways of integrating parse tree and word information (parallel, hierarchical and mixed). Other works have focused on integrating syntax in the decoder or through multi-task learning. Thus, [11] defines machine translation as a sequence-to-dependency task in which the decoder generates both words and a linearized dependency tree while [9] propose a scheduled multi-task learning approach where the main task is translation but the model is alternatively trained on POS tag, Dependency Tree and translation sequences.

Our model for syntax-aware summarization is similar to [12] in that we use a hierarchical model to integrate syntax in the encoder. We depart from it in that (i) we enrich the input with POS tag and/or dependency information rather than constituency parse trees; (ii) we apply our model to summarization rather than translation.

RL Sequence Models: Various RL models have been proposed for sequence-to-sequence models. [18] introduce an adaptation of REINFORCE [27] to sequence model and a curriculum learning strategy to alternate between ground truth and the sample from the RL model. This vanilla REINFORCE is known to have high variance. Thus, a learned baseline is equipped to mitigate this issue. [1] propose another reinforcement learning model, namely actor-critic, to have lower variance of model estimations, offsetting by a little bias. The impact of the bias, as well as the goodness of the model, relies particularly on the careful design of the *critic*. In practice, to ensure convergence, intricate techniques must be used including an additional target network Q', delayed actor, a critic value penalizing term and reward shaping. In contrast, [19] introduce a very simple and effective way to construct a better baseline for REINFORCE, namely self-critical sequence training (SCST) method. Instead of looking for and constructing a baseline or using a real critic as above, SCST uses its own prediction normally used at inference time to construct the sequence and uses this to normalize the reward. [10] adapt this training method to improve the abstraction of text summarization via a combination of cross-entropy, policy learning, pretrained language model and novel phrase reward. Similarly, we use SCST to train a summarization model. However, our model uses ROUGE as a reward and we focus on comparing models trained using different learning strategies (RL vs Cross Entropy) and informed by different sources (with and without syntax).

3 Models

We train and compare models that differ along two main dimensions: training (cross-entropy vs. RL) and syntax (with and without syntactic information).

3.1 Baseline

The baseline is a sequence-to-sequence model consisting of a bidirectional LSTM encoder and a decoder equipped with and an attention and a copy pointer-generator mechanism.

Encoder. The source sentence is encoded using two recurrent neural networks (denoted *bi-RNN*) [7]: one reads the whole sequence of words $x = (x_1, ..., x_m)$ from left to right and the other from right to left. This results in a forward and backward sequence of hidden states $(\overrightarrow{h_1}, ..., \overrightarrow{h_m})$ and $(\overleftarrow{h_1}, ..., \overleftarrow{h_m})$ respectively. The representation of each source word x_j is the concatenation of the hidden states $h_j = [\overrightarrow{h_j}, \overleftarrow{h_j}]$.

Decoder. An RNN is used to predict the target summary $y = (y_1, ..., y_n)$. At each decoder timestep, a multi-layer perceptron (MLP) takes as input the recurrent hidden state s_i, the previously predicted word y_{i-1} and a source-side context vector c_i to predict the target word y_i. c_i is the weighted sum of the source-side vectors $(h_1, ..., h_m)$. The weights in this sum are obtained with an attention model [2], which computes the similarity between the target vector s_{i-1} and every source vector h_j.

Copy-Pointer. The attention encoder-decoder tends to ignore the presence of rare words in the source, which might be important especially for the summarization task. The Copy-Pointer [22] enables to either copy source words via a pointer or generate words from a fixed vocabulary. A soft switch p_{gen} is learned to choose between *generating* a word from the vocabulary by sampling from the output distribution of the decoder, or *copying* a word from the input sequence by sampling from the attention distribution.

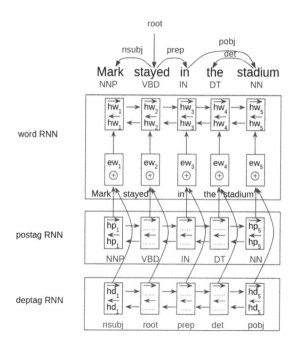

Fig. 1. Pos+Deptag model

3.2   Integrating Syntax

Conventional neural summarization models only rely on the sequence of raw words and ignore syntax information. We include syntactic information in our summarization model using the hierarchical-RNN topology introduced by [12] and comparing three sources of information: POS tags (Postag), dependency relations (Deptag) and their combination (Pos+Deptag). Figure 1 shows a graphical depiction of the Pos+tag model. In essence, each source of information (sequence of tokens, of POS tags, of dependency relations) is encoded using a bidirectional LSTM and each input token is then represented by the concatenation of the hidden-states produced by each information source considered. For instance, in the Postag model, the POS tag bi-LSTM takes as input a sequence of POS tags and outputs a sequence of hidden states $\left(hp_j = [\overleftarrow{hp_j}; \overrightarrow{hp_j}]\right)_{1 \leq j \leq m}$ similarly to the word bi-RNN. Each hp_j is then concatenated with the input word embeddings ew_j and passed on to the word bi-RNN.

For the Deptag model, the input sequence to the Deptag bi-LSTM includes, for each input tokens, the name of the dependency relation that relates this token to its syntactic head (e.g., *nsubj* for the token "Mark" in the sentence shown at the top of Fig. 1). The Deptag bi-LSTM then output a sequence of hidden states $\left(hd_j = [\overleftarrow{hd_j}; \overrightarrow{hd_j}]\right)_{1 \leq j \leq m}$ which are concatenated with the corresponding word embeddings ew_j and passed to the word bi-RNN.

Finally, for the Pos+Deptag model, both the POS tag and the syntactic hidden states are concatenated with the words embeddings to give the final input vector $[\overleftarrow{ew_j}; \overrightarrow{ew_j}; \overleftarrow{hp_j}; \overrightarrow{hp_j}; \overleftarrow{hd_j}; \overrightarrow{hd_j}]$ which is passed on to the upper-level word bi-RNN.

3.3   RL Learning

Summarization as an RL Problem. Neural summarization models are traditionally trained using the cross entropy loss. [18] propose to directly optimize Natural Language Processing (NLP) metrics by casting sequence generation as a Reinforcement Learning problem. As most NLP metrics (BLEU, ROUGE, METEOR,...) are non-differentiable, RL is appropriate to reach this objective. The parameters θ of the neural network define a *natural policy* p_θ, which can be used to predict the next word. At each iteration, the decoder RNN updates its internal state (hidden states, attention weights, copy-pointer weights...). After generating the whole sequence, a reward $r(\cdot)$ is computed, for instance the ROUGE score. This reward is evaluated by comparing the generated sequence and the gold sequence. The RL training objective is to minimize the negative expected reward:

$$L^{RL}(\theta) = -\mathbb{E}_{w^s \sim p_\theta}[r(w^s)] \tag{1}$$

where $w^s = (w_1^s, \ldots w_T^s)$ and w_t^s is the word sampled from the decoder at time step t. Following [27], the gradient $\nabla_\theta L^{LR}(\theta)$ can be computed as follows:

$$\nabla_\theta L^{RL}(\theta) = -\mathbb{E}_{w^s \sim p_\theta}[r(w^s)\nabla_\theta \log p_\theta(w^s)] \tag{2}$$

In practice, the vanilla REINFORCE yields a very high variance during training. In order to help the model stabilize and converge to good local optima, vanilla REINFORCE is extended to compute the reward *relative* to a *baseline* b:

$$\nabla_\theta L^{RL}(\theta) = -\mathbb{E}_{w^s \sim p_\theta}[(r(w^s) - b)\nabla_\theta \log p_\theta(w^s)] \tag{3}$$

This baseline can be an arbitrary function (function of θ or t), as long as it does not depend on w^s [25].

Self-critical Sequence Training. There are various ways to reduce RL variance and choose a proper baseline: for instance, using a second decoder [18] or building a *critic network* and optimizing with a *value network* instead of real reward [1]. In the following, we have chosen the self-critical sequence training (SCST) technique [19], which has been shown to be very simple and effective. The main idea of SCST is to use, as baseline in the vanilla REINFORCE algorithm, the reward obtained with the inference algorithm used at test time. Equation 3 then becomes:

$$\nabla_\theta L^{RL}(\theta) = -\mathbb{E}_{w^s \sim p_\theta} \left[(r(w^s) - r(\hat{w})) \nabla_\theta \log p_\theta(w^s) \right] \tag{4}$$

where $r(\hat{w})$ is the reward obtained by the current model with the inference algorithm used at test time. As demonstrated by [29], we can rewrite this gradient formula as:

$$\frac{\partial L^{RL}(\theta)}{\partial s_t} = (r(w^s) - r(\hat{w}))(p_\theta(w_t | w^s_{t-1}, h_t) - 1_{w^s_t}) \tag{5}$$

where s_t is the input to the final softmax function in the decoder. The term on the right side resembles logistic regression, except that the ground truth w_t is replaced by sampling w^s_t. In logistic regression, the gradient is the difference between the prediction and the actual 1-of-N representation of the target word:

$$\frac{\partial L^{XENT}(\theta)}{\partial s_t} = p_\theta(w_t | w_{t-1}, h_t) - 1_{w_t} \tag{6}$$

We see that samples that return a higher reward than $r(\hat{w})$ will be encouraged while samples that result in a lower reward will be discouraged. Therefore, SCST intuitively tackles well the exposure bias problem as it forces to improve the performance of the model with the inference algorithm used at test time. In order to speed up sequence evaluation at training time, we use greedy decoding with $\hat{w}_t = \arg\max_{w_t} p(w_t \mid h_t)$.[1]

Training Objective and Reward. The number of words in the vocabulary may be quite large in text generation, which leads to a large state space that may be challenging for reinforcement learning to explore. To reduce this effect, we follow [10] and adopt a final loss that is a linear combination of the cross-entropy loss and the policy learning loss:

$$L = (1 - \alpha)L^{XENT} + \alpha L^{RL} \tag{7}$$

α is a hyper-parameter that is tuned on the development set.

We use ROUGE-F_1 as the reward for the reinforce agent as the generation should be as concise as the gold target sentence.

---

[1] Two variants of this training method exist: TD-SCST and the "True" SCST, but both variants do not lead to significant additional gain on image captioning [19]. So we didn't explore these two variants for summarization as greedy decoding already obtains quite good result. We leave this for future work.

4 Experiments

Data. We evaluate our approach on the Gigaword corpus [20], a corpus of 3.8M sentence-headline pairs and where the average input sentence length is 31.4 words (in the training corpus) and the average summary length is 8.3 words. The test set consists of 1951 sentence/summary pairs. As [20], we use 2000 sample pairs (among 189K pairs) as development set.

Automatic Evaluation Metric. We adopt ROUGE [13] for automatic evaluation. It measures the quality of the summary by computing overlapping lexical units between the candidate and gold summaries. We report ROUGE-1 (unigram), ROUGE-2 (bi-gram) and ROUGE-L (longest common sequence) F1 scores. ROUGE-1 and ROUGE-2 mainly represent informativeness while ROUGE-L is supposed to be related to readability [4].

Implementation. Our models implementations are based on the Fast-Abs-RL [6] code[2]. Although this code is not optimized to give the best possible performances, it is flexible enough to allow for the integration of syntactic features.

The hyperparameter α in Eq. 7 needs careful tuning. Figure 2 illustrates a problematic case when α continuously increases until it reaches $\alpha = 1$ at iteration 10^5, where the RL models forget the previously learned patterns and degenerate. A good balance between exploration and supervised learning is thus necessary to prevent such catastrophic forgetting. We have found on the development set that the Reinforcement Learning weight α may increase linearly by (step/10^5) with the number of training iterations, until it reaches a maximum of 0.82 for the RL-s2s model and of 0.4 for the RL-s2s-syntax model.

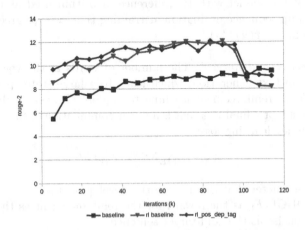

Fig. 2. Catastrophic forgetting of the RL decoder on the Gigaword dev set

---

[2] https://github.com/ChenRocks/fast_abs_rl.

For all models, we use the Adam optimizer [8] with a learning rate of 0.001 (tuned on the dev set). The word vocabulary size is 30k, number of part-of-speech tags 40 and number of dependency tags 244. We have chosen the default size (from the codebase) of 128 for word embeddings, and arbitrarily 30 dimensions both for the part-of-speech and dependency embeddings. Similarly, we have chosen the default values of 256 hidden states for every bidirectional RNN, 32 samples for the batch size, a gradient clipping of 2 and early-stopping on the development set. Our adapted code is given as supplementary material and will be published with an open-source licence (https://urldefense.proofpoint.com/v2/url?u=https-3A_github.com_lethienhoa_Eval-2DRL&d=DwIFaQ&c=vh6FgFnduejNhPPD0fl_yRaSfZy8CWbWnIf4XJhSqx8&r=8pdeajTECkGg7IiCE2coz4KdRwElEr3FQX_jYRdcVprH4Ev8v5ZWCYnpPJWwDKNa&m=skCykr24ZzAbXX_ByjZShMdeUYW0lScwb7cSw94vVaA&s=Rg87ZVRv7NYiy0TvRIplAYA_6g0GxTWSvcOWbriEYbw&e).

Table 1. Performance comparisons between models

Models	#Params	Time for 1 epoch	R-1	R-2	R-L
Re3Sum [3]	–	–	37.04	19.03	34.46
Our Baseline s2s	6.617M	13h18m	27.57	10.29	26.02
Postag s2s	+312k	+54m	30.52	12.13	28.8
Deptag s2s	+318k	+1h13m	30.25	12.15	28.73
Pos+Deptag s2s	+630k	+1h34m	30.8	12.3	29.22
RL s2s	+0	−1h35m	29.94	11.64	28.54
RL postag s2s	–	–	30.82	12.19	29.12
RL deptag s2s	–	–	30.58	12.08	29.01
RL pos+deptag s2s	–	–	30.76	12.31	29.11

5   Results and Analysis

ROUGE. Table 1 shows the performances measured in ROUGE score. State-of-the-art summarization system come from [3], which appears to be the best system on the Gigaword corpus reported in http://nlpprogress.com/english/summarization.html, as of May 2019.

Both Syntactic and RL models outperform the baseline.

Syntax-aware models outperform the baseline by +1.84 (Postag), +1.86 (Deptag) and +2.01 (Dep+Postag) ROUGE-2 points.

While RL without syntax slightly under-performs syntactic models, it still achieves an improvement of +1.35 rouge-2 over the baseline. In other words, directly optimizing the ROUGE metric helps improve performance almost as much as integrating syntactic information. The combination of reinforcement learning with syntax information keeps increasing the score. However, the resulting improvement is smaller than when adding syntax without RL. We speculate that because the search space with syntax has a larger number of dimensions than without syntax, it may also be more difficult to explore with RL.

Parameters. The baseline model has 6.617M parameters. This is increased by roughly 300K paramters for the Postag and the Deptag model and correspondingly by roughly 600K paramters for the Pos+Deptag model. In comparison, RL optimization does not involve any additional parameters. However, it requires two more decoder passes for the sampling and greedy predictions.

Speed. Syntax-aware models are slightly longer to train than the baseline. Running on a single GPU GeForce GTX 1080, the baseline model requires 13h18m per epoch with 114k updates while the training time of syntax-aware models increases by about 6% (Postag s2s). Also, it takes one week to get the preprocessing tag labels of these syntactic features for the whole 3.8M training samples of Gigaword corpus on 16 cores cpu machine Dell Precision Tower 7810. Surprisingly, adding the RL loss (which requires re-evaluating the ROUGE score for every generated text at every timestep) reduces training time by 12%. We speculate that the RL loss may act as a regularizer by smoothing the search space and help gradient descent to converge faster.

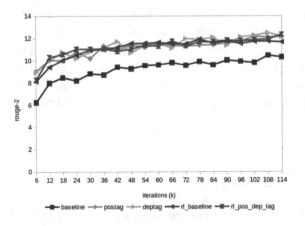

Fig. 3. Evolution on test set during training

Learning Curve. Figure 3 shows the evolution of Rouge-2 on the test set over 1 epoch. We can observe that syntactic models obtain a better performance than the baseline after the first 6k iterations. Sequence models with RL also quickly reach the same performance than syntactic models, even though the RL loss is only weakly taken into account at the start of training. As learning continues, the gap between the top models (with syntax and/or RL) and the baseline stays constant. The increased speed of training with RL, especially at the beginning of training, constitutes an important advantage in many experimental conditions.

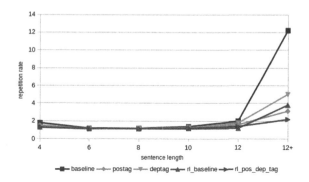

Fig. 4. Repetition comparisons by length (lower is better)

Repetitions. Repetition is a common problem for sequence-to-sequence models [21, 26]. To assess the degree of repetitions in the generated summaries, we use [11]'s repetition rate metric which is defined as follows:

$$rep\_rat = \sum_{i=1}^{T(y)} \frac{1 + r(\widetilde{y}_i)}{1 + r(Y)} \qquad (8)$$

where $\widetilde{y}_i$ and Y_i are the ith generated sentence and i^{th} gold abstract target sentence respectively, and r is the number of repeated words: $r(X) = len(X) - len(set(X))$. $len(X)$ is the length of sentence X and $len(set(X))$ is the number of words that are not repeated in sentence X. Figure 4 compares the repetition rate of several models; the horizontal axis is the length of sentences, and the vertical axis is the repetition rate. The proposed RL-model combined with syntactic information performs the best on long sentences, with less repeated words than all other models. Indeed, short sentences are less likely to contain repetitions, but it is interesting to observe that RL-training enriched with syntax improves the quality of long sentences on this aspect.

Analysis by Postags. To further investigate the linguistic structure of the generated output, we compute for each POS tag class T, the proportion of POS tags of type T relative to the number of generated words (on the test set). We group POS tags into 9 classes: cardinal numbers (CD), determiners (DT), nouns and proper nouns (NN), verbs (VV), adjectives (JJ), adverbs (RB), to (TO), prepositions and subordinating conjunctions (IN) and symbols (SYM).

We evaluate whether the generated summary has a similar or different POS tags distribution than the ground truth by computing for each model the mean square error (MSE) between every generated and gold POS tag class. These errors are shown in Table 2.

Table 2. Proportion of generated postags

Models	Content words				Function words					MSE to gold
	NN	VV	JJ	RB	CD	DT	TO	IN	SYM	to gold
Gold target	49	12.5	12.9	1.6	1.3	1.5	2.5	10.6	4	0
Our baseline s2s	43.4	13.8	10.8	1.4	1.3	1.6	3.5	8.9	11.3	10.52
Postag s2s	50.4	14.5	12.1	1.3	1.3	1.1	3.9	8.1	2.1	2.07
Deptag s2s	49.8	14.5	12	1.7	1.3	1.1	3.7	8.9	1.9	1.59
Pos+Deptag s2s	51.4	14.7	12.6	1.6	1.1	1	3.7	7.9	1.8	2.72
RL s2s	50	14.1	11.9	1.3	1.6	1.2	4.1	9.1	1.6	1.71
RL pos+deptag s2s	49.9	14.3	12.4	1.3	1.5	1.2	3.6	9	2.2	1.28

On average and for all POS tag classes, both syntax-aware and RL models are much closer (about 5 times) to the gold than the baseline. In a similar way as with repetitions, the best summarization model in terms of POS tag classes is the combined RL and syntax model.

Effects on Long Sentences. We group sentences of similar lengths together and compute the Rouge score. Figure 5 reports the Rouge-2 scores for various lengths of generated texts, with a 95% *t-distribution* confidence interval. It shows that the RL and syntax models perform globally better than the baseline as sentences get longer. For long sentences (more than 10 words), this effect is more pronounced, the syntax(+RL) models outperform significantly the RL and baseline models.

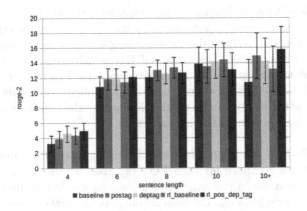

Fig. 5. Performance comparisons by length

Human Evaluation. In order to evaluate the quality of the summaries produced by the models, we asked 3 annotators to assess the relevance and grammaticality quality of the summaries. Each criterion is rated with a score from 0 (bad) to 5 (excellent). Annotators are instructed to evaluate 50 samples randomly selected from the test set. The model information is anonymous to the annotators. The evaluation results with a 95% *t-distribution* confidence interval is shown in Table 3. We see that RL performs on par with postag, deptag on relevance and grammaticality criterions and they all outperfom baseline. This is consistent with the results on POS tag classes above which indicate that these models generate more content words and less function words than the baseline. Once again, RL with pos+deptag obtains the best result.

Table 3. Human evaluations

Models	Rel.	Grammar.
Baseline s2s	2.13 (±0.14)	2.47 (±0.18)
Postag s2s	3.26 (±0.18)	4.19 (±0.16)
Deptag s2s	3.17 (±0.19)	4.2 (±0.17)
RL s2s	3.23 (±0.19)	4.26 (±0.16)
RL pos+deptag	3.45 (±0.18)	4.49 (±0.13)

Qualitative Analysis. Table 4 shows some sample outputs of several models. Example 1 presents a typical repetition problem (the word *"atlantis"*) often found in the baseline. Both syntax and RL models manage to avoid repetitions. Example 2 shows that RL (without any syntactic information) can search and find surprisingly the same structure as the syntax-aware model. In the last example, the baseline fails as it stops accidentally after a modal verb while syntax and RL models can successfully generate well-formed sentences with subject-verb-object. However, semantically, RL and RL with pos+dep tag (like the baseline model) fail to capture the true meaning of the gold summary (*"transport plane"* instead of *"air force"* should be the real subject in this case). Deptag s2s seems the best in terms of summarizing syntactic and semantic content on these examples.

Table 4. Generated examples of different models.

Source	The us space shuttle atlantis separated from the orbiting russian mir space station early saturday, after three days of test runs for life in a future space facility, nasa announced
Abstract	Atlantis mir part ways after three-day space collaboration by emmanuel unk
Baseline s2s	*Atlantis atlantis atlantis separated from mir space station*
Postag s2s	Us space shuttle atlantis separated from mir space station
Deptag s2s	Atlantis separated from russian space station
Rl s2s	Us shuttle atlantis separated from mir
Rl pos+deptag s2s	Us shuttle atlantis separated from russian space station
Source	Swedish telecommunications giant ericsson has reached a basic agreement to sell its relay production to japanese electronics company UNK corp, ericsson said thursday
Abstract	Ericsson sells relay production to unk's unk corp
Baseline s2s	*Ericsson to sell its its to sell its*
Postag s2s	Ericsson to sell relay production to unk
Deptag s2s	Ericsson reaches basic agreement to sell relay production
Rl s2s	Ericsson reaches basic agreement to sell relay production
Rl pos+deptag s2s	Ericsson sells relay production to unk corp
Source	The shooting down of the largest transport plane in the sri lankan air force has wrecked supply lines and slowed a major government offensive against the tamil rebel citadel of jaffna, analysts said
Abstract	Downing of plane slows sri lanka's army onslaught on jaffna by amal jayasinghe
Baseline s2s	*Sri lankan air force has*
Postag s2s	Sri lankan air force plane shooting down
Deptag s2s	Sri lanka's largest transport plane shooting kills supply lines
Rl s2s	Sri lankan air force wrecked supply lines
Rl pos+deptag s2s	Sri lankan air force shooting down

6   Conclusion

We have studied in details in this work the quality of syntactic implication of the summaries that are generated by both syntactically-enriched summarization models and reinforcement-learning trained models, beyond the traditional ROUGE-based metric classically used to evaluate summarization tasks. We have thus focused on the quality of the generated summaries, in terms of the number of repeated words, which is a common issue with summarization systems, but also in terms of the distribution of various types of words (through their POS-tags) as compared to the gold. Because these aspects strongly depend on sentence length, we have also studied the impact of sentence length. Finally, we have manually evaluated the quality of the generated sentences in terms of relevance and grammaticality. Our results suggest that enriching summarization models with both syntactic information and RL training improves the quality of generation in all of these aspects. Furthermore, when computational complexity is a concern, we have shown that RL-only models may be a good choice because they provide nearly as good results as syntactic-aware models but with less parameters and faster convergence time. We plan to extend this work by further applying similar qualitative evaluations to other types of summarization models and text generation tasks.

Acknowledgments. This work has been funded by Lorraine Université d'Excellence; experiments realized in this work have beendone partly on Grid5000 Inria/Loria Nancy. We would like to thank all consortiums for giving us access to their resources.

References

1. Bahdanau, D., et al.: An actor-critic algorithm for sequence prediction. CoRR abs/1607.07086 (2016). http://arxiv.org/abs/1607.07086
2. Bahdanau, D., Cho, K., Bengio, Y.: Neural machine translation by jointly learning to align and translate. arXiv e-prints abs/1409.0473, September 2014
3. Cao, Z., Li, W., Li, S., Wei, F.: Retrieve, rerank and rewrite: soft template based neural summarization. In: Proceedings of the 56th Annual Meeting of the Association for Computational Linguistics (Volume 1: Long Papers), Melbourne, Australia, pp. 152–161. Association for Computational Linguistics, July 2018. https://www.aclweb.org/anthology/P18-1015
4. Cao, Z., Wei, F., Li, W., Li, S.: Faithful to the original: fact aware neural abstractive summarization. In: Proceedings of the Thirty-Second AAAI Conference on Artificial Intelligence, (AAAI 2018), the 30th innovative Applications of Artificial Intelligence (IAAI 2018), and the 8th AAAI Symposium on Educational Advances in Artificial Intelligence (EAAI 2018), New Orleans, Louisiana, USA, 2–7 February 2018, pp. 4784–4791 (2018). https://www.aaai.org/ocs/index.php/AAAI/AAAI18/paper/view/16121
5. Celikyilmaz, A., Bosselut, A., He, X., Choi, Y.: Deep communicating agents for abstractive summarization. In: Proceedings of the 2018 Conference of the North American Chapter of the Association for Computational Linguistics: Human Language Technologies, pp. 1662–1675 (2018)
6. Chen, Y.C., Bansal, M.: Fast abstractive summarization with reinforce-selected sentence rewriting. In: Proceedings of ACL (2018)
7. Chung, J., Gulcehre, C., Cho, K., Bengio, Y.: Empirical evaluation of gated recurrent neural networks on sequence modeling. In: NIPS 2014 Workshop on Deep Learning, December 2014 (2014)
8. Kingma, D.P., Ba, J.: Adam: a method for stochastic optimization. arXiv preprint arXiv:1412.6980 (2014)
9. Kiperwasser, E., Ballesteros, M.: Scheduled multi-task learning: from syntax to translation. Trans. Assoc. Comput. Linguist. **6**, 225–240 (2018)
10. Kryscinski, W., Paulus, R., Xiong, C., Socher, R.: Improving abstraction in text summarization. In: Proceedings of the 2018 Conference on Empirical Methods in Natural Language Processing, Brussels, Belgium, 31 October–4 November 2018, pp. 1808–1817 (2018). https://aclanthology.info/papers/D18-1207/d18-1207
11. Le, A.N., Martinez, A., Yoshimoto, A., Matsumoto, Y.: Improving sequence to sequence neural machine translation by utilizing syntactic dependency information. In: IJCNLP (2017)

12. Li, J., Xiong, D., Tu, Z., Zhu, M., Zhang, M., Zhou, G.: Modeling source syntax for neural machine translation. In: Proceedings of the 55th Annual Meeting of the Association for Computational Linguistics (Volume 1: Long Papers), Vancouver, Canada, pp. 688–697. Association for Computational Linguistics, July 2017. https://www.aclweb.org/anthology/P17-1064

13. Lin, C.Y.: ROUGE: a package for automatic evaluation of summaries. In: Marie-Francine Moens, S.S. (ed.) Text Summarization Branches Out: Proceedings of the ACL-04 Workshop, Barcelona, Spain, pp. 74–81. Association for Computational Linguistics, July 2004. http://www.aclweb.org/anthology/W04-1013

14. Nallapati, R., Zhou, B., dos Santos, C., Gulcehre, C., Xiang, B.: Abstractive text summarization using sequence-to-sequence RNNs and beyond. In: Proceedings of The 20th SIGNLL Conference on Computational Natural Language Learning, Berlin, Germany, pp. 280–290. Association for Computational Linguistics, August 2016. https://www.aclweb.org/anthology/K16-1028

15. Narayan, S., Cohen, S.B., Lapata, M.: Ranking sentences for extractive summarization with reinforcement learning. In: Proceedings of the 2018 Conference of the North American Chapter of the Association for Computational Linguistics: Human Language Technologies, Volume 1 (Long Papers), pp. 1747–1759. Association for Computational Linguistics (2018). http://aclweb.org/anthology/N18-1158

16. Pasunuru, R., Bansal, M.: Multi-reward reinforced summarization with saliency and entailment. In: Proceedings of the 2018 Conference of the North American Chapter of the Association for Computational Linguistics: Human Language Technologies, New Orleans, Louisiana, pp. 646–653 (2018)

17. Paulus, R., Xiong, C., Socher, R.: A deep reinforced model for abstractive summarization. In: Proceedings of the 6th International Conference on Learning Representations, Vancouver, BC, Canada (2018)

18. Ranzato, M., Chopra, S., Auli, M., Zaremba, W.: Sequence level training with recurrent neural networks. In: 4th International Conference on Learning Representations, ICLR 2016, Conference Track Proceedings, San Juan, Puerto Rico, 2–4 May 2016 (2016). http://arxiv.org/abs/1511.06732

19. Rennie, S.J., Marcheret, E., Mroueh, Y., Ross, J., Goel, V.: Self-critical sequence training for image captioning. In: 2017 IEEE Conference on Computer Vision and Pattern Recognition (CVPR), pp. 1179–1195 (2017)

20. Rush, A.M., Chopra, S., Weston, J.: A neural attention model for abstractive sentence summarization. In: Proceedings of the 2015 Conference on Empirical Methods in Natural Language Processing, pp. 379–389. Association for Computational Linguistics (2015). http://aclweb.org/anthology/D15-1044

21. Sankaran, B., Mi, H., Al-Onaizan, Y., Ittycheriah, A.: Temporal attention model for neural machine translation. CoRR abs/1608.02927 (2016)

22. See, A., Liu, P.J., Manning, C.D.: Get to the point: summarization with pointer-generator networks. In: Proceedings of the 55th Annual Meeting of the Association for Computational Linguistics (Volume 1: Long Papers), Vancouver, Canada, pp. 1073–1083. Association for Computational Linguistics, July 2017. https://www.aclweb.org/anthology/P17-1099

23. Sennrich, R., Haddow, B.: Linguistic input features improve neural machine translation. In: Proceedings of the First Conference on Machine Translation, Berlin, Germany, pp. 83–91. Association for Computational Linguistics, August 2016. https://www.aclweb.org/anthology/W16-2209

24. Sutskever, I., Vinyals, O., Le, Q.V.: Sequence to sequence learning with neural networks. In: Ghahramani, Z., Welling, M., Cortes, C., Lawrence, N.D., Weinberger, K.Q. (eds.) Advances in Neural Information Processing Systems, vol. 27, pp. 3104–3112. Curran Associates, Inc. (2014). http://papers.nips.cc/paper/5346-sequence-to-sequence-learning-with-neural-networks.pdf
25. Sutton, R.S., Barto, A.G.: Reinforcement Learning: An Introduction. MIT Press (1998). http://www.cs.ualberta.ca/~sutton/book/the-book.html
26. Tu, Z., Lu, Z., Liu, Y., Liu, X., Li, H.: Modeling coverage for neural machine translation. In: Proceedings of the 54th Annual Meeting of the Association for Computational Linguistics (Volume 1: Long Papers), Berlin, Germany, pp. 76–85. Association for Computational Linguistics, August 2016. https://www.aclweb.org/anthology/P16-1008
27. Williams, R.J.: Simple statistical gradient-following algorithms for connectionist reinforcement learning. Mach. Learn. **8**, 229–256 (1992)
28. Xu, W., Napoles, C., Pavlick, E., Chen, Q., Callison-Burch, C.: Optimizing statistical machine translation for text simplification. Trans. Assoc. Comput. Linguist. **4**, 401–415 (2016)
29. Zaremba, W., Sutskever, I.: Reinforcement learning neural turing machines. CoRR abs/1505.00521 (2015)
30. Zhang, X., Lapata, M.: Sentence simplification with deep reinforcement learning. In: Proceedings of EMNLP (2017)

Dependable Neural Networks for Safety Critical Tasks

Molly O'Brien[1,2]([✉]) [iD], William Goble[1] [iD], Greg Hager[2] [iD],
and Julia Bukowski[3] [iD]

[1] exida LLC, Sellersville, PA 18960, USA
{mobrien,wgoble}@exida.com
[2] Department of Computer Science, Johns Hopkins University,
Baltimore, MD 21218, USA
hager@cs.jhu.edu
[3] Department of Electrical and Computer Engineering, Villanova University,
Villanova, PA 19085, USA
julia.bukowski@villanova.edu

Abstract. Neural Networks are being integrated into safety critical systems, e.g., perception systems for autonomous vehicles, which require trained networks to perform safely in novel scenarios. It is challenging to verify neural networks because their decisions are not explainable, they cannot be exhaustively tested, and finite test samples cannot capture the variation across all operating conditions. Existing work seeks to train models robust to new scenarios via domain adaptation, style transfer, or few-shot learning. But these techniques fail to predict how a trained model will perform when the operating conditions differ from the testing conditions. We propose a metric, Machine Learning (ML) Dependability, that measures the network's probability of success in specified operating conditions *which need not be the testing conditions*. In addition, we propose the metrics Task Undependability and Harmful Undependability to distinguish network failures by their consequences. We evaluate the performance of a Neural Network agent trained using Reinforcement Learning in a simulated robot manipulation task. Our results demonstrate that we can accurately predict the ML Dependability, Task Undependability, and Harmful Undependability for operating conditions that are significantly different from the testing conditions. Finally, we design a Safety Function, using harmful failures identified during testing, that reduces harmful failures, in one example, by a factor of 700 while maintaining a high probability of success.

Keywords: Machine learning testing and quality · Neural network dependability · Neural network safety · Reinforcement Learning

1 Introduction

Neural Networks are being integrated into safety critical, cyber-physical systems, e.g., object detection for autonomous vehicles [6]. Relying on learned networks

© Springer Nature Switzerland AG 2020
O. Shehory et al. (Eds.): EDSMLS 2020, CCIS 1272, pp. 126–140, 2020.
https://doi.org/10.1007/978-3-030-62144-5_10

to automate safety critical tasks requires robust network evaluation. Neural Networks (hereafter referred to as *networks*) make decisions that are not explainable. Most networks cannot be exhaustively tested. Recent work shows that network performance can be brittle and change with minimal changes to the input data distributions [12]. It is unclear how to predict a network's performance in an untested scenario; thus, it is unclear how to predict a network's performance in untested operating conditions.

1.1 Training Robust Networks

The Machine Learning (ML) community is actively researching techniques to train models robust to unseen scenarios via domain adaptation, style transfer, or few-shot learning. Prior work has also investigated how to ensure safety *during* network training [14,18].

Domain Adaptation. Domain adaptation seeks to adjust a trained network to new operating domains. See [3] for a survey of visual domain adaptation techniques. RoyChowdhury et al. propose a method to leverage unlabeled data in a new operating domain to fine-tune a trained network [13]. RoyChowdhury et al. show an increase in pedestrian detection over baseline for a network trained using sunny images from the Berkely Deep Drive Dataset (BDD100K) [17] and adapted to rainy, overcast, snowy day, and night images. Liu et al. address Open Domain Adaptation (generalizing to an unseen target domain) and Compound Domain Adaptation (generalizing to combined target domains) [8]. Liu et al. demonstrate results on a compound target of rainy, cloudy and snowy and an open target of overcast images.

Style Transfer. In perception, style transfer is used to render images from one domain as if they were from another. Style transfer can be used in safety critical tasks to render a novel scenario in a known style. CycleGANs have achieved impressive results rendering photographs as if they were painted by different artists and transferring the style of similar animals, e.g., rendering a horse as a zebra [19]. Gong et al. extend CycleGANs for continuous style generation flowing from one domain to another [5]. Gong et al. demonstrate results transferring styles between object detection datasets.

Few-Shot and Zero-Shot Learning. Few-shot (zero-shot) learning aims to learn a task for given operating conditions with little (no) labeled training data. James et al. use a task embedding to leverage knowledge from previously learned, similar tasks [7] and demonstrate that a robot can learn new tasks with only one real-world demonstration. See [16] for a survey of zero-shot learning.

1.2 Software Dependability

Software dependability is defined in [2] as "a system's ability to avoid service failures that are more frequent and more severe than acceptable". Initial work improving the Dependability of ML models proposed testing-based approaches to estimate the performance of software when no testing-oracle is available [10].

1.3 Adaptive Network Testing

Automated test case generation is often necessary in software verification, because most software cannot be tested exhaustively. See [1] for an orchestrated survey of automated testing techniques. Adversarial techniques can be used to identify catastrophic failures in networks performing safety critical tasks [15]. Recent work evaluated autonomous vehicles by selecting test scenarios along boundaries where the model's performance changed quickly [9]. Mullins et al. parameterized the testing space by possible variations in the mission and environment and defined test outcomes by mission success or failure and safety success or failure.

1.4 Our Contributions

In ML, network performance is typically measured by the probability of success. We propose that *how* a network fails can be as important as the probability a network will succeed. Specifically, we distinguish between failures that do not violate safety constraints, which we call task failures, and failures that violate safety constraints (whether or not the task is completed), which we call harmful failures.

In this work, we propose the performance of a network is described by the fraction of successes, task failures, and harmful failures for a given task in specified conditions. To the best of our knowledge, we tackle the previously unaddressed problem: how to evaluate network performance and safety *after* training is complete, when the operating conditions differ from the testing conditions. The contents of this paper are as follows:

1. We define ML Dependability[1] as the probability of completing a task without harm. We define Task Undependability and Harmful Undependability to distinguish failures by the consequences: task failures causing no harm as opposed to harmful failures.
2. We develop mathematics to predict the model performance in novel operating conditions by *re-weighting* known test results with knowledge of the novel operating condition probabilities.
3. We accurately predict the ML Dependability, Task Undependability, and Harmful Undependability of a network trained to perform a simulated robot manipulation task in novel operating conditions using test results.
4. We design a Safety Function to reduce harmful failures in the simulated robot manipulation task under testing conditions. We reduce the harmful failures, in one example, by a factor of 700 while maintaining a high probability of success.
5. We discuss how this work can be translated to practical applications and describe directions for future work.

---

[1] This is distinct from software Dependability defined in [2].

2   Methods

Table 1. Notation

π	The trained Neural Network
X	The set of all possible domain scenarios
x	A domain scenario. $x \in X$
$\pi(x)$	Success indicator for π in scenario x
$\pi_{avg}(r_d)$	The average value of $\pi(x)$ for scenarios x in region r_d
$\pi^T(x)$	Task failure indicator for π in scenario x
$\pi^H(x)$	Harmful failure indicator for π in scenario x
τ	The testing conditions
O	The operating conditions
$P_\tau(X), P_O(X)$	The probability distribution describing all possible scenarios during testing, operation (respectively)
$p_\tau(x), p_O(x)$	The probability of encountering scenario x during testing, operation (respectively)
$D_O(\pi)$	The dependability of π in conditions O
$U_O^T(\pi)$	The task undependability of π in conditions O
$U_O^H(\pi)$	The harmful undependability of π in conditions O
v	The obstacle velocity [inches/second] in the robot simulation experiments
t	The obstacle start time [seconds] in the robot simulation experiments
y	The robot goal position [inches] in the robot simulation experiments

2.1   Machine Learning Dependability

See Table 1 for the notation used in this paper. In this work we evaluate the performance of a trained, deterministic neural network, π, performing a safety critical task. A **domain scenario**, x, is defined as one set of environment conditions and goals for the network. A network may be used iteratively within one scenario, e.g., a controller moving a robot incrementally towards a goal, or used once, e.g., a classifier labelling a sensor reading as valid or faulty. For each scenario, the network attempts to complete a task without causing harm. The outcome of deploying a network in a scenario is the observed **behavior mode**. We define three behavior modes: success, task failure, and harmful failure. A network is successful if it accomplished the task without causing harm. A task failure occurs when the network failed to complete the specified task but did not cause harm. Any scenario where the network caused harm is labeled a harmful failure, whether or not the task was completed. The **domain space**, X, of a network describes the set of possible domain scenarios. A fully-observed domain includes all variables in the environment and system which impact the outcome of the network. A partially-observed domain includes a subset of the full domain. The **input space** of a network is defined as the information the network observes. When a network is deployed iteratively, it may observe many inputs for one scenario. The input may include components of the domain space, but need not include the entire domain space. Domain spaces may be numerical or categorical. Note that for a fully-observed numerical domain, one domain scenario x maps to exactly one behavior mode[2].

We indicate the success of running network π in scenario x as $\pi(x)$. $\pi(x) = 1$ when the model is successful in scenario x; $\pi(x) = 0$ when the model has a task or harmful failure. π is tested with N sampled scenarios $\{x_n\}_{n=1}^N$, $x_n \sim P_\tau(X)$ where $p_\tau(x_n)$ describes the probability of encountering scenario x_n during testing. We define **Machine Learning Dependability** as the probability that a model will succeed when operated under specified conditions. We aim to estimate $D_O(\pi)$: the ML Dependability of model π deployed under the operating conditions described by $P_O(X)$, where $P_O(X) \neq P_\tau(X)$[3].

For this analysis, it is assumed that the domain space is numerical and fully observed, that $P_\tau(X)$ and $P_O(X)$ are known, and that while $P_O(X) \neq P_\tau(X)$, both distributions have the same domain space X.

2.2   Derivation

Discrete-Bounded Domain Space. To begin, we assume X is discrete with finite D possible values, $X = \{x_d\}_{d=1}^D$. The probability distribution describing scenarios during testing is:

$$P_\tau(X) = \{p_\tau(x_1), ..., p_\tau(x_D)\} = \{p_\tau(x_d)\}_{d=1}^D \tag{1}$$

The probability distribution describing scenarios during operation is:

$$P_O(X) = \{p_O(x_d)\}_{d=1}^D \tag{2}$$

Note that $P_\tau(X)$ and $P_O(X)$ can be estimated without testing or operating the network. *As a motivating example, imagine a perception network for an*

---

[2] $\pi(x)$ can map to multiple values if x does not fully describe the variables that impact the success of the model, i.e., the domain is partially-observed. We define the domain space for modalities like images or speech as partially observed, because many different pixel-values or spectrographs can represent a specified label (a tree in the rain, a man saying "hello world"). When $\pi(x)$ cannot be modeled as a constant value, it may be modeled as a distribution. Extending this work to partially-observed domains is an important challenge we hope to address in future work.

[3] The ML Dependability of π under testing conditions, $D_\tau(\pi)$, is equal to the network accuracy or the fraction of successful tests: $D_\tau(\pi) = \sum_{i=1}^N \frac{\pi(x_i)}{N}$. Likewise, $U_\tau^T(\pi) = \sum_{i=1}^N \frac{\pi^T(x_i)}{N}$ and $U_\tau^H(\pi) = \sum_{i=1}^N \frac{\pi^H(x_i)}{N}$.

autonomous vehicle. The perception network is trained and tested in Palo Alto but will operate in Seattle. Information like weather patterns can be used to estimate the probability of different scenarios during testing and operation without recording or labelling data in the testing or operating conditions.

The ML Dependability of network π operating in conditions O is defined as the probability that model π succeeds when deployed in a scenario x randomly sampled from the operating conditions $x \sim P_O(X)$. This is computed as the expected value of $\pi(x)$, for $x \sim P_O(X)$.

$$D_O(\pi) = E[\pi(x)], \quad x \sim P_O(X) \tag{3}$$

$$D_O(\pi) = \sum_{d=1}^{D} p_O(x_d) * \pi(x_d) \tag{4}$$

$P_O(X)$ is known. $\pi(x_d)$ must be evaluated via testing. The reader is reminded that the network is fixed and it is assumed the domain space is numerical and fully observed, so $\pi(x_d)$ is 1 or 0 for a unique x_d. If the domain space of the network is truly discrete and $D < \infty$, then the network can be exhaustively tested with D tests. (Note, if D is finite but large it may be infeasible to exhaustively test the network. This case may be treated as discrete-unbounded.) In most applications, the domain space is discrete-unbounded or continuous so the network cannot be tested exhaustively.

Discrete-Unbounded or Continuous Domain Space. We approximate discrete-unbounded or continuous domain spaces as discrete-bounded by partitioning X into D partitions, with $D < \infty$. Let the dth partition be defined as the contiguous region r_d of X, such that $\cup_{d=1}^{D} r_d = X$. The reader is reminded that N test scenarios are drawn from $P_\tau(X)$ as $\{x_n\}_{n=1}^{N}$. N_d scenarios lie in each partition where $\{x_i^d\}_{i=1}^{N_d}$ denotes the scenarios in partition d. We require the partitions are defined so that at least one test scenario lies within each partition, $N_d > 0, \forall d \in [0, D]$. $P_O(X)$ is equivalently described by:

$$P_O(X) = \{p_O(r_d)\}_{d=1}^{D} \tag{5}$$

where $p_O(r_d)$ is computed as: $p_O(r_d) = \sum_{x_n \in r_d} p_O(x_n)$ for discrete-unbounded domains, or $p_O(r_d) = \int_{r_d} p_O(x)dx$ for continuous domains[4]. $\pi_{avg}(r_d)$ can be estimated as:

$$\pi_{avg}(r_d) \approx \frac{\sum_{i=1}^{N_d} \pi(x_i^d)}{N_d} \tag{6}$$

The overall ML Dependability can now be approximated as:

$$D_O(\pi) \approx \sum_{d=1}^{D} p_O(r_d) * \pi_{avg}(r_d) \tag{7}$$

$$D_O(\pi) \approx \sum_{d=1}^{D} p_O(r_d) * \frac{\sum_{i=1}^{N_d} \pi(x_i^d)}{N_d} \tag{8}$$

---

[4] Note, x is not required to be one dimensional.

Estimating Undependability. In a similar manner, we can estimate the undependability of the model π in the operating conditions O. $\pi^T(x) = 1$ when the task is not completed but no harm is done, and $\pi^T(x) = 0$ otherwise. The **Task Undependability**, $U_O^T(\pi)$, is the probability that the model will fail to complete the desired task without causing harm in conditions O. We compute the Task Undependability as:

$$U_O^T(\pi) = E[\pi^T(x)], \quad x \sim P_O(X) \tag{9}$$

$$U_O^T(\pi) \approx \sum_{d=1}^{D} p_O(r_d) * \frac{\sum_{i=1}^{N_d} \pi^T(x_i^d)}{N_d} \tag{10}$$

$\pi^H(x) = 1$ in the event of a harmful failure, and is zero otherwise. The **Harmful Undependability** of the model, $U_O^H(\pi)$, is the probability that the model will cause harm when operated in conditions O, whether or not the task is completed. The Harmful Undependability is computed as:

$$U_O^H(\pi) = E[\pi^H(x)], \quad x \sim P_O(X) \tag{11}$$

$$U_O^H(\pi) \approx \sum_{d=1}^{D} p_O(r_d) * \frac{\sum_{i=1}^{N_d} \pi^H(x_i^d)}{N_d} \tag{12}$$

Note that success, task failure, and harmful failure are mutually exclusive, so $D_O(\pi) + U_O^T(\pi) + U_O^H(\pi) = 1$.

3   Experiments

We evaluated the performance of a Neural Network agent trained via Reinforcement Learning to move a simulated robot in the presence of an obstacle that moves at a constant velocity, v, starting at time t. The obstacle moves from right to left in the scene with its bottom edge 25 in. from the robot base. The robot's task is to reach or exceed a goal position, y, while avoiding the obstacle, see Fig. 1. The domain space, X, is defined as $v \in [0, 10]$ inches/second, $t \in [0, 10]$ seconds, and $y \in [0, 50]$ inches. The domain space X is bounded, continuous, and fully observed. The robot starts at 0 in. and is constrained to be within [0, 50] inches[5]. The simulations last 100 s and the network moves the robot forward 5 in. or back 5 in. every second. The robot moves for the entire 100 s simulation, even after the goal position is reached. A simulation only terminates before 100 s if the robot collides with the obstacle.

To succeed, the robot must reach or exceed the goal position before the end of the simulation and avoid the obstacle for the entire simulation. A simulation is a task failure if the robot does not reach the goal position but avoids collision with the obstacle. Any simulation where the robot collides with the obstacle is

---

[5] If the robot tries to move outside this region, the position is clipped. There is no penalty for trying to move outside the valid region.

Robot Manipulation Task

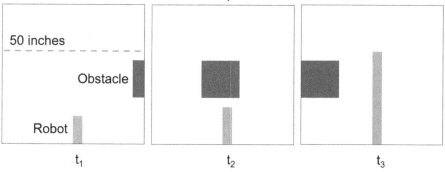

Fig. 1. The simulated robot manipulation task. To succeed, the robot must avoid the obstacle, which moves at a constant velocity v from right to left, starting at time t, and reach or exceed a goal location, y, between 0 and 50 in. t_1: the obstacle has started moving. t_2: the robot is avoiding collision with the obstacle. t_3: the robot has successfully reached and/or exceeded its goal position without colliding with the obstacle.

a harmful failure. In the following results, the behavior modes are denoted with the following colors: success is indicated with green, task failure with blue, and harmful failure with pink.

The network consists of two linear layers separated by a Rectified Linear Unit (ReLU) and is trained using a modified version of the PyTorch Q-Learning tutorial [11]. Each second, the network observes the position of the obstacle, the position of the robot, the speed of the obstacle, and the robot goal. Timing information is not input to the network. Zero-mean Gaussian noise with a standard deviation of 0.1, 0.1, 0.5 for $v, t,$ and y respectively is added to the inputs to simulate sensor noise. The reward function for the network was designed so reaching the goal resulted in a reward of 30 points and colliding with the obstacle resulted in a penalty of -50 points. Before reaching the goal position, the network received a small reward of 5 points for moving towards the goal or a penalty of -5 points for moving away from the goal. Before the obstacle had passed the robot, the network received a reward of 2 points for each time step it was below the obstacle and a penalty of -2 points each time step it was in the path of the obstacle. The point values for reaching the goal ($+30$ points) and collision (-50 points) were chosen to prioritize safety over task completion. Likewise, the intermediate rewards were chosen so that moving towards the goal (± 5 points) was prioritized above a potential, future collision (± 2 points).

3.1   Performance During Testing

X is a bounded, continuous domain space. We sample 100,000 test scenarios uniformly from the domain space:

$$P_\tau(X) : v \sim U(0, 10), t \sim U(0, 10), y \sim U(0, 50)$$

where $U(a, b)$ indicates a uniform probability distribution from a to b. We deployed the trained network in each test scenario to evaluate the network performance. The network had an ML Dependability of **90.35%**, a Task Undependability of **4.18%**, and a Harmful Undependability of **5.47%**. See Fig. 2 for a plot of observed failures by test scenario.

Task failures (shown in blue in Fig. 2) occurred when the obstacle speed was less than or equal to 0.80 in./s. Inspection revealed that the network learned to wait for the obstacle to pass before moving forward. In many cases the robot moved as far forward as it could, exceeding the input robot goal. When the obstacle moved very slowly, this strategy did not give the network enough time to reach the goal. Harmful failures (shown in pink in Fig. 2) occurred when the robot goal was greater than or equal to 38.47 in.

We partition each dimension of the domain space into 10 equal regions to obtain 1,000 voxels in domain space. v and t are divided into regions 1 in./s and 1 s wide (respectively). y is divided into regions 5 in. wide. We use these voxels to predict the model performance in new operating conditions.

3.2   Predicting Model Performance in Novel Operating Conditions

We demonstrate that our method can predict the performance of a network when deployed in novel operating conditions. We define four novel operating

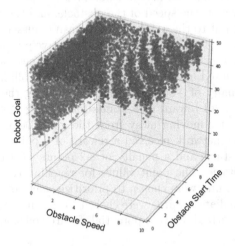

Fig. 2. The observed failures during testing, best viewed in color. Blue indicates a task failure. Pink indicates a harmful failure. The task failures (along the left 'wall' of the figure) occurred when the obstacle speed was less than or equal to 0.80 in./s. The harmful failures (along the 'ceiling' of the figure) occurred when the robot goal was greater than or equal to 38.47 in. (Color figure online)

conditions in Fig. 3, left. The harmful failures in testing occurred for robot goals greater than or equal to 38.47 in. We selected Operating Conditions 1 to simulate safe conditions: $y \in [0, 30]$ inches. Operating Conditions 2 simulate dangerous conditions: $y \in [30, 50]$ inches. We also wanted to select distributions other than uniform (the testing distribution) to make the prediction task more challenging. We selected Operating Conditions 3 to introduce a Gaussian domain distribution and focus the obstacle velocity v towards slower speeds to target the area where task failures occurred. Operating Conditions 4 are the most challenging to predict with Gaussian distributions in v and y focused towards observed task failures and harmful failures.

We used the partitions defined in Subsect. 3.1 to predict the model performance. To confirm our predictions, 100,000 simulations were run for each set of operating conditions. A comparison of our predicted network performance with the observed performance is shown in Fig. 3, above. We accurately predicted the ML Dependability, Task Undependability, and Harmful Undependability within 2% of observed results.

3.3 Performance with a Safety Function

Testing revealed that harmful failures only occurred with robot goals greater than or equal to 38.47 in. We designed a Safety Function to reduce harmful failures by clipping the robot goal input to the network to be between $[0, 38.47 - \delta]$

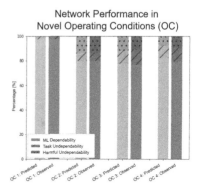

	Obstacle Speed v	Obstacle Start Time t	Robot Goal y
OC 1	$U(0,10)$	$U(0,10)$	$U(0,30)$
OC 2	$U(0,10)$	$U(0,10)$	$U(30,50)$
OC 3	$\mathcal{N}(3,2^2)$	$U(0,10)$	$U(30,50)$
OC 4	$\mathcal{N}(3,2^2)$	$U(0,10)$	$\mathcal{N}(35,10^2)$

Fig. 3. Predicted and observed performance of the trained network in Novel Operating Conditions (OC). **Left:** OC Specification. $\mathcal{N}(\mu, \sigma^2)$ denotes a Gaussian with a mean of μ and a standard deviation of σ. The sampled scenarios $x \sim \mathcal{N}(\mu, \sigma^2)$ are clipped to lie within the specified domain X. $x < X.min$ is set to $X.min$ and $x > X.max$ is set to $X.max$. t is not listed because $t \sim U(0, 10)$ for all conditions. **Right:** Predicted and observed performance of the trained network in OCs. OC predicted performance shown left in light colors. Observed performance shown right in bold colors. ML Dependability $D_O(\pi)$ is shown as solid green, Task Undependability $U_O^T(\pi)$ is shown as blue hatched, and Harmful Undependability $U_O^H(\pi)$ is shown as pink dotted bars. (Color figure online)

inches. We chose $\delta = 0.5$ inches. The reader is reminded that the network continues to move the robot after the goal position is reached, until the simulation ends at 100 s. Clipping the robot goal *input* to the network was intended to make the network behave more conservatively[6]; it was still possible for the robot to exceed the clipped goal and reach the original goal position. The Safety Function did not change the conditions for success: for a simulation to be successful the robot had to reach the original goal position. 100,000 new test scenarios were sampled from the Testing Conditions and run with the Safety Function. With the Safety Function, the network had a ML Dependability of **95.19%**, a Task Undependability of **4.81%**, and a Harmful Undependability of **0.007%**. Figure 4, above, offers a side-by-side comparison of observed failures and network performance with and without the Safety Function.

4   Discussion

4.1   Robot Manipulation Task

We see in Fig. 2 that the network performance varies by region in the domain space. Partitioning the domain space enables these regional variations to emerge when we predict the network performance in novel operating conditions.

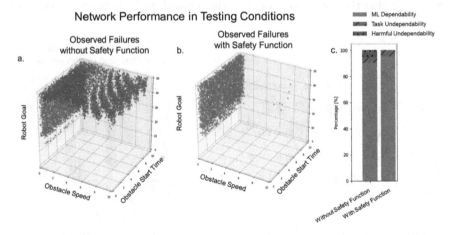

Fig. 4. A comparison of the network performance without the Safety Function and with the Safety Function, best viewed in color. Task failures are indicated in blue. Harmful failures are indicated in pink. (a) a reprint of Fig. 2 to facilitate comparison. (b) the observed failures in Testing Conditions with the Safety Function. (c) a comparison of the network ML Dependability, Task Undependability, and Harmful Undependability with and without the Safety Function. Note, the Harmful Undependability is reduced from 5.47% to 0.007% with the Safety Function. (Color figure online)

---

[6] This is a similar idea to Control Governors [4].

Overall, we accurately predict the performance of the network in novel operating conditions. Across the four proposed operating conditions and three performance metrics, the error between the predicted and observed performance percentage was within 2%. The prediction is poorer for Gaussian domain spaces as compared to uniformly distributed domain spaces. Finer partitioning of the domain space would lead to better predictions and may be necessary as domain space distributions become more complex.

The Safety Function reduced the number of harmful failures by a factor of 700. Surprisingly, even though our Safety Function clipped the input robot goal, it converted many harmful failures into successes. Clipping the robot goal made the network behave more conservatively, i.e. the network waited for the obstacle to pass before moving as far forward as it could. In general, we expect Safety Functions to reduce the probability of harmful failures, but we do not expect them to increase the probability of success. Our Safety Function was hand-crafted, but in the future, Safety Functions can be learned. It may also be desirable to design or learn different Safety Functions for different operating conditions. Targeted Safety Functions could prove a scalable approach for ensuring safety in dynamic environments, and may be more feasible than retraining the network for different operating conditions.

Understanding the Network's Behavior. Both failure modes of the network, task failure and harmful failure, relate to timing. The current time step was not an input to the network; subsequently the network did not learn to make decisions based on timing. The network ML Dependability could be improved in the future by adding a timing input.

Task failures occurred when the obstacle speed was less than or equal to 0.80 inches per second. The network learned to wait for the obstacle to pass the robot before moving past the obstacle, towards the goal. When the obstacle moved slowly this strategy did not give the robot enough time to reach the goal. But, in these scenarios the network had ample time to reach the robot goal *before* the obstacle passed the robot. Adding a timing input could allow the network to learn more sophisticated timing strategies.

Harmful failures occurred when the robot goal was greater than or equal to 38.47 in. The network learned an incorrect trade-off between moving towards the goal and avoiding the obstacle. The Safety Function results, see Fig. 4, reveal that in most of the scenarios that were harmful failures in testing, the robot had enough time to avoid collision and reach the goal before the end of the simulation. But the strategy learned by the network did not time the robot's approach correctly. Interestingly, the reward function was specifically designed to weight safety over task completion: a collision resulted in a penalty of -50 points whereas reaching the goal resulted in a reward of 30 points. While we do not claim that it would be impossible to craft a reward function to perfectly complete this task without harm, this example illustrates that designing a reward function that appropriately weights task requirements and safety constraints is not trivial. Safety Functions are an explainable alternative to hand crafting reward functions and guarantee a degree of safety for a network.

4.2   Dependable Networks in Practical Applications

We make several key assumption in our analysis. The implications of these assumptions determine how this work can be applied in practical applications. We assume that the domain space is numerical. Many applications have numerical domains such as force sensors and distance sensors, e.g. lidar.

We assume the domain is fully observed. A domain space may be fully observed in a constrained, industrial setting. But as learned networks move into unconstrained, dynamic environments, it is not possible to assume the domain space is fully observed. In partially observed domain spaces, the key change is that we do not assume one scenario x maps to exactly one output. When we modeled discrete-unbounded and continuous fully observed domain spaces, we modeled the performance of a network in a regions as $\pi_{avg}(r_d)$. This can be extended in the future to model the distribution of outcomes observed from scenario x when the domain is only partially observed. The quality of the performance predictions will vary by how well the partially observed domain describes the full domain. Adequate domain coverage requires expert knowledge. Choosing the dimensions by which we model the domain is an existing challenge and is a direction for further research. Another challenge in modeling practical domain spaces is *the curse of dimensionality*: as the dimension of the domain space grows, the number of partitions or regions can grow prohibitively large. We believe this challenge can be overcome in the future by either selectively choosing the domain to focus on the critical modes of variation for the given application, or leveraging similar scenarios 'across' domain variations to limit the effective dimension of the domain space.

We assume $P_\tau(X)$ and $P_O(X)$ are known. As stated earlier, $P_\tau(X)$ and $P_O(X)$ can be estimated empirically from statistical data or domain knowledge. Lastly, we assume both distributions cover the same domain space X and that the number of test samples in each partition is greater than zero. This assumption requires some care when designing the partitions.

4.3   Future Work

In the future we hope to investigate methods to automatically partition the domain space and to estimate the confidence intervals for predicted ML Dependability, Task Undependability, and Harmful Undependability using the number of samples available in each partition. A rich direction for future research is extending this work to partially-observed domains such as perception. Safety in partially-observed domain spaces is particularly relevant for technology like autonomous vehicles.

5   Conclusions

We define and derive the metrics ML Dependability, Task Undependability, and Harmful Undependability to predict a trained network's performance in novel operating conditions. We demonstrate that our metrics can predict the performance of a trained network in novel operating conditions within 2% of observed performance for a simulated robot manipulation task. We designed a hand-crafted Safety Function to avoid harmful failures identified during testing; the Safety Function was demonstrated to reduce harmful failures by a factor of 700.

Acknowledgments. We would like to acknowledge exida LLC for supporting this work. We would like to thank Mike Medoff, Chris O'Brien, André Roßbach, and Austin Reiter for their helpful discussions.

References

1. Anand, S., et al.: An orchestrated survey of methodologies for automated software test case generation. J. Syst. Softw. **86**(8), 1978–2001 (2013)
2. Avizienis, A., Laprie, J.C., Randell, B., Landwehr, C.: Basic concepts and taxonomy of dependable and secure computing. IEEE Trans. Dependable Secure Comput. **1**(1), 11–33 (2004)
3. Csurka, G.: Domain adaptation for visual applications: a comprehensive survey. arXiv preprint arXiv:1702.05374 (2017)
4. Garone, E., Di Cairano, S., Kolmanovsky, I.: Reference and command governors for systems with constraints: a survey on theory and applications. Automatica **75**, 306–328 (2017)
5. Gong, R., Li, W., Chen, Y., Gool, L.V.: DLOW: domain flow for adaptation and generalization. In: Proceedings of the IEEE Conference on Computer Vision and Pattern Recognition, pp. 2477–2486 (2019)
6. Grigorescu, S., Trasnea, B., Cocias, T., Macesanu, G.: A survey of deep learning techniques for autonomous driving. arXiv preprint arXiv:1910.07738 (2019)
7. James, S., Bloesch, M., Davison, A.J.: Task-embedded control networks for few-shot imitation learning. arXiv preprint arXiv:1810.03237 (2018)
8. Liu, Z., et al.: Compound domain adaptation in an open world. arXiv preprint arXiv:1909.03403 (2019)
9. Mullins, G.E., Stankiewicz, P.G., Hawthorne, R.C., Gupta, S.K.: Adaptive generation of challenging scenarios for testing and evaluation of autonomous vehicles. J. Syst. Softw. **137**, 197–215 (2018)
10. Murphy, C., Kaiser, G.E.: Improving the dependability of machine learning applications (2008)
11. Paszke, A.: Reinforcement learning (dqn) tutorial. https://pytorch.org/tutorials/intermediate/reinforcement_q_learning.html
12. Recht, B., Roelofs, R., Schmidt, L., Shankar, V.: Do CIFAR-10 classifiers generalize to CIFAR-10? arXiv preprint arXiv:1806.00451 (2018)
13. RoyChowdhury, A., et al.: Automatic adaptation of object detectors to new domains using self-training. In: Proceedings of the IEEE Conference on Computer Vision and Pattern Recognition, pp. 780–790 (2019)

14. Turchetta, M., Berkenkamp, F., Krause, A.: Safe exploration in finite Markov decision processes with Gaussian processes. In: Advances in Neural Information Processing Systems, pp. 4312–4320 (2016)
15. Uesato, J., et al.: Rigorous agent evaluation: an adversarial approach to uncover catastrophic failures. arXiv preprint arXiv:1812.01647 (2018)
16. Wang, W., Zheng, V.W., Yu, H., Miao, C.: A survey of zero-shot learning: settings, methods, and applications. ACM Trans. Intell. Syst. Technol. (TIST) **10**(2), 13 (2019)
17. Yu, F., et al.: BDD100K: a diverse driving video database with scalable annotation tooling. arXiv preprint arXiv:1805.04687 (2018)
18. Zhang, Y., Balkcom, D., Li, H.: Towards physically safe reinforcement learning under supervision. arXiv preprint arXiv:1901.06576 (2019)
19. Zhu, J.Y., Park, T., Isola, P., Efros, A.A.: Unpaired image-to-image translation using cycle-consistent adversarial networks. In: The IEEE International Conference on Computer Vision (ICCV), October 2017

Author Index